JUST JESUS

SEE HIM. LIVE HIM. HEAR HIM. LOVE HIM.

A 52 WEEK DEVOTIONAL

WRITTEN BY:
STEPHEN WILLIS
MIKE LYLE

DESIGNED BY:
CALEB ATKINS

This book was made possible with the effort and generosity of these people:

Rick and Debbie Huff
Cavan and Soni Carlton
Doug and Nancy Fry
Lee and Tonja Hall
Emily Heady
Rachael Kamm
Nick Willis

We are eternally grateful.

To request permissions, contact the publisher at info@leaddeep.org

Paperback: ISBN 978-1-7359143-0-5
Ebook: ISBN 978-1-7359143-1-2

Library of Congress Control Number: 2020921260

First paperback edition November 2020.

Edited by Emily Heady and Rachael Kamm
Cover art, layout and design by Caleb Atkins
All Photographs used with permission from www.unsplash.com
Illustrations licensed from stockunlimited.com

All Scripture quotations are from the NIV translation unless otherwise noted.

Printed by Lead Deep in the United States of America

Lead Deep
110 Wyndview Drive
Lynchburg, VA 24502

Leaddeep.org

CONTENTS

Welcome   7

How to use this Guide   8

JANUARY - THE IDENTITY OF JESUS

Week One - Jesus as Creator   12   Week Three - Jesus as Our Friend   25
Week Two - Jesus as God's Beloved Son   18   Week Four - Jesus as our Brother   32

FEBRUARY - THE SEEDS OF JESUS

Week One - Jesus as Strong Warrior   38   Week Three - Jesus as Faithful Love   52
Week Two - Jesus as Redeemer   45   Week Four - Jesus as Deliverer   58

MARCH - THE SACRIFICE OF JESUS

Week One - Jesus as the Lamb   64   Week Three - Jesus as Suffering Servant   77
Week Two - Jesus as the Offering   71   Week Four - Jesus as our Peace   83

APRIL - THE HOPE OF JESUS

Week One - Jesus as the Champion   89   Week Three - Jesus as our Hope   102
Week Two - Jesus as the Gardener   96   Week Four - Jesus as the Treasure   108

MAY - THE WAY OF JESUS

Week One - Jesus as the Way   114   Week Three - Jesus as the Truth   127
Week Two - Jesus as the Invitation   121   Week Four - Jesus as the Life   133

JUNE - THE POWER OF JESUS

Week One - Jesus as the Power to Witness   139   Week Three - Jesus as Power to Live a Holy Life 151
Week Two - Jesus as the Power to Belong   145   Week Four - Jesus as the Power to See   158

JULY - THE INVITATION OF JESUS

Week One - Jesus as Captain   164   Week Three - Jesus as the Fisher of Men   176
Week Two - Jesus as Guide   170   Week Four - Jesus as the Legacy   182

AUGUST - THE COMPASSION OF JESUS

Week One - Jesus as our Vision   188   Week Three - Jesus as Compassion   200
Week Two - Jesus as our Filter   194   Week Four - Jesus and our Model   206

SEPTEMBER - THE CONFRONTATION OF JESUS

Week One - Jesus as Prophet 213 Week Three - Jesus as Sword-Bringer 22'

Week Two - Jesus as Teacher 220 Week Four - Jesus as the Dividing Force 23:

OCTOBER - THE GOODNESS OF JESUS

Week One - Jesus as Lord 240 Week Three - Jesus as Cheerleader 253

Week Two - Jesus as the Treasure 247 Week Four - Jesus as Promise Keeper 259

NOVEMBER - THE MIRACLES OF JESUS

Week One - Jesus as Healer 265 Week Three - Jesus as the Gospel 27'

Week Two - Jesus as the Finger of God 272 Week Four - Jesus as the Authority 28.

DECEMBER - THE PRESENCE OF JESUS

Week One - Jesus as the Promised One 290 Week Three - Jesus as the Nazarene 30:

Week Two - Jesus as Emmanuel 296 Week Four - Jesus as King 308

5TH WEEKS

Water that Drowns - Jesus as New Creation 315

Water that Parts - Jesus and Trusting God 321

Water that Names - Jesus as Personal 327

Water that's Gone - Jesus as Tempted 333

WELCOME

It seemed like it would be just a normal Saturday breakfast meeting at Cracker Barrel. I had shown up that day—I thought—to catch up with a Brazilian missionary friend who was passing through town. I had expected that I would hear about his ministry and that he would hear about mine, that we'd pray for each other, find ourselves encouraged, and go about our business. But as I left the meeting, I knew that the truth I had gleaned there had already begun to transform me.

What was this truth? Be careful—it's so simple, it's easy to miss! Here it is: the Christian life is all about Jesus. This simple truth can and should change the way we live. How do we do that? For starters, we might want to take stock of all the extra things—the non-Jesus things—around which we have focused our Christianity. Many of them are good things—ministries, projects, sermons, music, small groups. But sometimes these good things can clutter and complicate the real thing: our relationship with Jesus. If they don't bring abundant life, then they are distractions and we need to set them aside.

What if we focused entirely on Jesus and nothing but Jesus? How would that change things? I left that meeting with a new passion within my soul to pray, plan, and preach only Jesus. When we long to See Him, Hear Him, Love Him, and Live Him, we open ourselves to a life of abundance. It truly is all about Jesus!

We understand that the world probably doesn't need another devotional. But the world does need Christians who are practiced at seeing Jesus, living like Jesus, listening to Jesus, and loving Jesus. When we learn to do all these things, Jesus is lifted up and people are drawn to Him. Jesus is the point, the main attraction, the model, and the goal. He is the source of the abundant life that we all long for.

This devotional should be seen as an invitation to orient your life around Jesus and only Jesus. I know this can be hard to do. We live crowded lives, and figuring out how to hear His voice in the middle of all the noise can be challenging. But there are things we can do to help you hear Him. Any musician, no matter how great, must tune his instrument and listen for the beat if he's to help create a symphony. In fact, the better the musician, the better he typically is at playing in step with others—and it takes years of practice to get there. We, too, need to practice tuning our ears to hear Jesus and pacing our steps to match His rhythms. This year is your invitation to practice: you can commit to focus your life on seeing, living like, listening to, and loving the source of life and it to the full: Jesus.

HOW TO USE THIS GUIDE

Beach vacations are great—family, water, relaxation. I love sunsets at the beach: they're bright, almost shocking, and so easy to enjoy. You just have to notice when they come, and they can make your dinner of boardwalk French fries feel so much more special.

Sunrises are different: they're easier to miss, and you have to be purposeful about seeing them—they come early, right when it would feel really nice to stay in bed! When I do manage to catch the sunrise at the beach, though, I never regret it. The morning sun seems to take the stage like a great conductor in nature's orchestra, calling the whole world to attention as it rises above the ocean. Its muted pastels, like the quiet opening bars of a symphony, take my breath away, and the anticipation builds.

If I want to participate in this experience, I have to arrange my day to make it happen, just as I would for an appointment I need to keep. I have to plan to set my body to the rhythm of the sun.

What if Jesus is more like a sunrise than a sunset? It would mean that if we are going to focus on Him, we need to be deliberate about it—to adopt habits that help us to give Him our full attention and to set our own lives to the rhythm of the Son. This devotional is written with that purpose in mind.

We have provided four large movements of three months, which loosely follow the Christian Calendar. The purpose of this is to provide a Jesus-rhythm for the whole year:

SEE HIM · LIVE HIM · HEAR HIM · LOVE HIM

Each month establishes a different perspective on ways that we can see, hear, live, and love Jesus under the larger theme of the quarterly movement. Within this framework, you are invited to sync up your life to a smaller, weekly rhythm that puts you in step with Jesus. This may sound confusing, but don't worry—you don't have to memorize it. The point is that throughout the year, as you work through this devotional, you will be practicing the movements that can help you pay attention to and sync your life up with Jesus. Sometimes there will be repetition, just as there is if you are learning to play an instrument or a sport. And sometimes you may find that some movements come a lot more easily to you than others. This is normal! You're learning, and God has your timing well under His control. Just rest in these rhythms and let them transform you as they have me.

What is the best way to do this? I would love for you to engage in these rhythms with other people, but I also know there are times when that is not possible or practical. So, this devotional is written with flexibility in mind: You can use it with a small group or by yourself.

For those of you who like to know what you're getting into, here are snapshots of the both the large and small rhythms we will be trying to establish. Large rhythms are the four ways we want to approach focusing on Jesus (See Him, etc.), with some smaller specific applications for each. Small themes are the tasks or habits you adopt for each day of the week to drive home those large rhythms. They're your practice space.

LARGE RHYTHM:

 Identity of Jesus, Seeds of Jesus, Sacrifice of Jesus

 The Hope of Jesus, The Way of Jesus, the Power of Jesus

 The Invitation of Jesus, The Compassion of Jesus, The Confrontation of Jesus

 The Goodness of Jesus, the Miracles of Jesus, the Presence of Jesus

SMALL RHYTHM:

SUNDAY	MONDAY	TUESDAY
Worship with a community of believers	Read Scripture and pray.	Read the Scripture and the short devotional thought, and pray.

WEDNESDAY	THURSDAY	FRIDAY	SATURDAY
Read the Scripture and engage in a spiritual practice.	Read the Scripture and engage in some deepening questions.	Read the Scripture and reflect on the week.	Rest.

More specifically, here is what your practice drills will consist of:

Scripture (**Monday - Friday**): Each week will have one portion of Scripture that will be the focus for the entire week. This, along with prayer, will be the dominant tool we will use to establish a Jesus-rhythm. The Scriptures are alive and can provide new insights every time we engage them. Some days you may learn something and other days you may be just reading. This is OK. Just present yourself to the Scriptures every day, releasing any pressure you may feel for them to "do" anything for you.

Commentary (**Tuesday**): These are short devotionals that are meant to help you think about the Scriptures in new ways that relate back to our large rhythms. The hope is to help shine a spotlight on Jesus in the Scriptures. Some of these will resonate strongly for you, and others may not seem all that relevant. That is also OK—just listen and give God the space to reveal what He wants to show you.

Spiritual Practice (**Wednesday**): Over the centuries, the Church has noticed the power of certain disciplines to focus the disciple on the transforming power of Jesus in them. We have selected 12 practices and invited you to practice one each month throughout the year.

Deepening Questions (Thursday): Often, Jesus taught by utilizing good questions. They invite us to chew on new ideas and force us to think about how these ideas play out in our everyday lives. The questions provided in this guide can be used as journal prompts or as small group questions.

Reflection (Friday): God has given us many ways to know Him better. For example, the beauty of a painting could stop us in our tracks and force us to pay attention—or we might glance at it and go on with our day. The call for reflection is the call to stop and pay attention to what you are seeing. These reflection times invite you to do this through activities like freewriting, drawing, creating something, or just sitting and remembering what God has done for you.

Rest (Saturday): Even God stopped producing and took some time to enjoy His creation. You are invited to simply enjoy God's creation-—your family, a bath, a hike, a good meal, etc. Or maybe you just need a nap!

> " The Christian life is **all about Jesus**. This simple truth can and should change the way we live. "

JANUARY - WEEK ONE

JESUS AS CREATOR

MONDAY - READ JOHN 1:1-18

know what you're thinking: it's going to be really fun to start a year of Jesus with the Christmas story. After all, most of the Gospels start that way—and who doesn't love the Christmas story? Let's go back to a different place, though—one that leads us not to see Jesus as a baby in a manger but as the creative force behind the entire universe.

This is where the Gospel of John begins: "In the beginning was the Word, and the Word was with God, and the Word was God." John's use of the phrase "in the beginning" sends us all the way back to Genesis, to the creation story. When God created the heavens and the earth, Jesus, the Word, was there. And not only was He there, but He was there as part of the Godhead: He was and is God. Just to be sure we get it, John then goes on to say that everything was made through Jesus. In the beginning, Jesus wasn't just watching; He was doing the work!

Why does it matter that the very first picture that John provides of Jesus is that of a creator? Maybe it's John's way of helping us know where to look for Him—we can't see Him, after all, if we are looking in the wrong place. Instead of looking past the angels and cows into the manger, then, let's look where Jesus first shows up: in the void, the very beginning of creation.

Most of us find it unpleasant to think about blankness and emptiness—but Jesus isn't afraid of the void. In fact, it's one of the places He's most able to work. If Jesus is the creator, then that makes Him (shocking!) creative! No one loves a blank canvas more than a master artist. And if He can make something beautiful out of nothing, then doesn't it make sense that Jesus can create genuinely new things out of your life?

Sometimes, though, we see our void as a prison that locks us into old patterns. Henri Nouwen articulates it well: "We allow our past, which becomes longer and longer each year, to say to us: 'You know it all; you have seen it all, be realistic; the future will be just another repeat of the past. Try to survive it as best you can.'" As you read this in the beginning of January, you may feel like you are in a chaotic void that can never produce anything new—just the same old mess. If Jesus is creative, though, each moment is pregnant with potential; every day is full of promise. In the beginning, Jesus made something out of nothing; He brought life out of the chaotic void. So, He can make something new out of you!

Will we receive Him? Will the creative Word of God take root in our lives?

Nouwen, Henri. *Here and Now: Living in the Spirit.* Crossroads Publishing Company. New York, NY. 1994. *Page 16*

MEDITATION

▼

*Psalm 1:1-2 "Blessed is the one who does not walk in step with the wicked or stand in the way that sinners take or sit in the company of mockers, but whose delight is in the law of the Lord, and who **meditates** on his law day and night."*

The Hebrew word that is translated as "meditate" in this psalm means to growl or mutter to oneself. The picture it would elicit in the mind of an ancient Israelite is one of a lion who is enjoying his meal. He chews on the food and growls to himself in delight as he moves the choice morsels around in his mouth. This seems gruesome, but it helps us to understand what it means to meditate. It is not merely emptying your mind. It is focusing your attention in a single direction as you take delight in Scripture. Meditating on Scripture means you read a small portion and say it over and over again in your mind. You pace yourself in the Scripture and take delight in the life it brings you.

This week, meditate on the words of Matthew 3:17: "And a voice from heaven said, 'This is my son, whom I love; in whom I am well pleased." Memorize this small Scripture as an anchor for the identity of Jesus. You can also imagine God saying these words to you: This is my son/daughter, whom I love, in whom I am well pleased. Try doing this imaginative exercise for five minutes, three times today.

▼

1. What does it mean to be creative?
2. Have you ever thought of Jesus as being creative? Why/Why not?
3. What changes in your relationship with Jesus when you see Him as creative/creator?
4. What needs to be created in you (Read Psalm 51:10)? Name a new pattern you are going to trust Jesus to make in your thinking or in your life.
5. John tells us that Jesus was not received by His own creation (John 1:10-11). Why did the world reject Jesus? Are those same tendencies active in your own life? Which ones?

Read John 1:1-18 and reflect on the week.
What has the Holy Spirit revealed to you this week?

SATURDAY | REST

"Be still and know that I am God." Psalm 46:10

JANUARY - WEEK TWO

JESUS AS SON OF GOD

MONDAY - READ MATTHEW 17:1-8

In this week's Scripture, Jesus turns to a few of his disciples and invites them to join Him on a mountaintop. Can you imagine what it felt like to get an invitation like that? These disciples weren't the first. Moses joined God the Father high up on a mountain in Exodus, where God revealed Himself to Moses and gave him the law. Moses was so affected by the encounter that his face glowed when he came back down! In I Kings, Elijah hears an invitation to go join God on a mountaintop. He does, and God reveals Himself to Elijah not as a force of infinite, fear-inducing power but as a still, small voice—an intimate friend who wants to talk. I would like you to hear that same invitation. Jesus wants you to join Him, as it's on mountaintops that He shows us more about Himself and invites us to know Him more intimately.

This story is usually referred to as the "transfiguration" because in it, Jesus is changed in such a way that His disciples are able to see Him for who He really is. There's a lot going on here, and it's going to take us a couple of weeks to unpack this story. This week, we will focus on the words that God the Father says, as they help the disciples understand what they were seeing: "This is my son, whom I love; with him I am well pleased." These are loaded words, and these Jewish disciples knew that "son of God" was a phrase that was already heavy with meaning.

> " Jesus wants you to join Him. On mountaintops He shows us more about Himself and invites us to know Him more intimately. "

Not surprisingly, the idea of the "son of God" goes all the way back to Genesis. In the beginning, God puts someone in the garden who bears His image and is meant to serve as a partner in bringing about His desired end for creation. Adam is a reflection of God in creation and therefore might be called a son of God. We all know the story, though. Adam fails to reflect God fully and creation falls into chaos. So God graciously offers humanity another chance as He selects a family (Israel) to accomplish the same purpose. He even calls Israel His firstborn son.

Exodus 4:22

But, again, this family fails in its holy vocation. It does not reflect God fully—as a son should—and so finds itself powerless and oppressed. God continues to deal graciously with His wayward sons, giving them Moses's law to follow and prophets like Elijah to help them keep on the right path. But with every opportunity, the reflection of God in man grows dimmer.

Eventually, there arises a hope that God Himself will provide someone to fulfill the role that Adam and Israel fail to fulfill. This person, the thinking goes, will be a perfect reflection of God and work fully in rhythm with God to bring about His will for creation. This character will fully live up to the identity of the "son of God." When the disciples hear Jesus called the "son of God," they know a prophecy is being fulfilled and all of humanity's hopes are coming to fruition.

Jesus will receive this holy vocation; He will perfectly reflect God in creation. All the other reflections are imperfect mirrors. But in Jesus, God decided to enter creation Himself. Thus, Jesus can be a visible image of the invisible God! This is what it means for Jesus to be called God's son. When we are looking at God, let's seek to see only Jesus, like the disciples at the end of this week's Scripture.

³ Isaiah 52:13-15

MEDITATION

▼

*Psalm 1:1-2 "Blessed is the one who does not walk in step with the wicked or stand in the way that sinners take or sit in the company of mockers, but whose delight is in the law of the Lord, and who **meditates** on his law day and night."*

The Hebrew word that is translated as "meditate" in this psalm means to growl or mutter to oneself. The picture it would elicit in the mind of an ancient Israelite is one of a lion who is enjoying his meal. He chews on the food and growls to himself in delight as he moves the choice morsels around in his mouth. This seems gruesome, but it helps us to understand what it means to meditate. It is not merely emptying your mind. It is focusing your attention in a single direction as you take delight in Scripture. Meditating on Scripture means you read a small portion and say it over and over again in your mind. You pace yourself in the Scripture and take delight in the life it brings you.

This week, meditate on the words of Matthew 3:17: "And a voice from heaven said, 'This is my son, whom I love; in whom I am well pleased." Memorize this small Scripture as an anchor for the identity of Jesus. You can also imagine God saying these words to you: This is my son/daughter, whom I love, in whom I am well pleased. Try doing this imaginative exercise for five minutes, three times today.

1. Do you believe that Jesus is God?
2. What changes in your relationship with Jesus if you believe He is God?
3. Do you believe that God is Jesus?
4. What changes in your understanding of what God is like if there is no un-Christlikeness in God?
5. Read Romans 8:14-17. What does it mean for you to be a son/daughter of God?

Read Matthew 17:1-8 and reflect on the week.
What has the Holy Spirit revealed to you this week?

SATURDAY | REST

*"Come to me, all you who are weary and burdened,
and I will give you rest." Matthew 11:28*

JANUARY - WEEK THREE

JESUS AS FRIEND

MONDAY - READ MATTHEW 17:6-8 AND JOHN 15:15

At my elementary school—and probably at yours too—there was a playground bully. During recess, he would send his cronies after the younger kids to catch them and make them bow down to him. I don't know why none of us thought to tell a teacher. Maybe we were just too busy running! This bully taught me an early life lesson: it's better to run away from some types of people. Good people bring out the best in us and give us a space in which to be ourselves; they make us want to come closer. Bad people make us feel insecure and small; they gloat when we bow down to them, and in fact, that's exactly what they seek.

In the scene of the transfiguration, where we're camped out for another week, the disciples seem to be having a playground moment. At the very least, they're bowing facedown! These disciples have every reason to want to hide: they have just heard the voice of God and they are afraid. They have not yet learned that God is not someone to run away from in fear (1 John 4:18).

> " The relationship Jesus wants to have with us, however, is far from long-distance! He wants to be close—so close He can touch us. "

We may not find ourselves literally facedown in front of Jesus. But we all know how the emotions of fear and uncertainty can overwhelm us. Sometimes, it seems like our natural posture toward God is like that of the disciples—the wrong kind of fear. We cower, assuming that He is angry and wants to punish us. If we lose our job, we assume God is chastising us for not doing it right. If some disaster strikes, we assume God is angry at some sin we have committed. Our enemy is very willing to reinforce these ideas. He says things like "God is displeased. God wants the worst for you. God is angry, upset, and disappointed with you." These words usually cause us to shrink back in fear and shame. Imagine yourself facedown, hiding, and terrified. That's how we feel when we assume that God is perpetually angry with us and out to get us.

But what is Jesus's response when we are paralyzed by fear? Let's look at how He responds to the disciples. If anyone has the right to gloat, punish, judge, or reject, it's Jesus. But instead of glorying in His dominance like a playground bully, Jesus reaches out to the disciples in friendship. He reaches out to us in friendship as well.

Jesus is a friend who speaks words of life. Jesus tells the disciples to "get up." The word He uses here is egiero - **cause to stand up, raise to life, restore**. This is the same word Jesus uses when he says that He must be raised to life after three days (Matthew 16:21). This is a resurrection word. When the disciples are paralyzed with fear, Jesus speaks words of LIFE.

When you're at your worst—LIFE! When you're defeated—LIFE! When your relationships are broken, you feel alone, and you're paralyzed by uncertainty—LIFE! LIFE! LIFE! You have a friend in Jesus who comes close, pulls you up out of fear, and speaks "egeiro." Get up. I'm here. Receive My love and live. Do you see Him as your friend?

MEDITATION

▼

*Psalm 1:1-2 "Blessed is the one who does not walk in step with the wicked or stand in the way that sinners take or sit in the company of mockers, but whose delight is in the law of the Lord, and who **meditates** on his law day and night."*

The Hebrew word that is translated as "meditate" in this psalm means to growl or mutter to oneself. The picture it would elicit in the mind of an ancient Israelite is one of a lion who is enjoying his meal. He chews on the food and growls to himself in delight as he moves the choice morsels around in his mouth. This seems gruesome, but it helps us to understand what it means to meditate. It is not merely emptying your mind. It is focusing your attention in a single direction as you take delight in Scripture. Meditating on Scripture means you read a small portion and say it over and over again in your mind. You pace yourself in the Scripture and take delight in the life it brings you.

This week, meditate on the words of Matthew 3:17: "And a voice from heaven said, 'This is my son, whom I love; in whom I am well pleased." Memorize this small Scripture as an anchor for the identity of Jesus. You can also imagine God saying these words to you: This is my son/daughter, whom I love, in whom I am well pleased. Try doing this imaginative exercise for five minutes, three times today.

▼

Can you describe a relationship that was bad for you? Why was it bad? Was that person a "friend" as most people would define friend? Why/Why not?

Are you afraid of God? Why?

Does it change your view of God if you think about Jesus as a friend? How so?

Read John 15:15. What does this mean to you?

Describe how you relate to someone who is or has been a true friend in your life. Can you use the same words to describe your relationship with Jesus? Why/Why not?

....

....

....

....

....

....

....

....

....

Read Matthew 17:1-8, John 15:15, and reflect on the week.
What has the Holy Spirit revealed to you this week?

SATURDAY | REST

"Come with me by yourselves to a quiet place and get some rest." Mark 6:31b

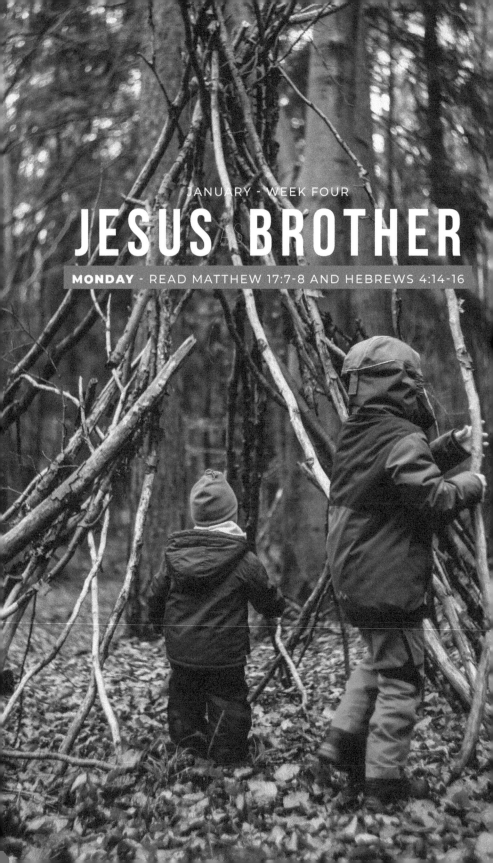

JANUARY - WEEK FOUR

JESUS as BROTHER

MONDAY - READ MATTHEW 17:7-8 AND HEBREWS 4:14-16

ast week, we saw Jesus inviting the disciples to come closer rather than shrinking ack in fear. Personally, I imagine He literally holds out a hand to them as He avites them to get up. How close does Jesus have to be to touch the disciples? ight: close. So why do we so often see Jesus as far away? Sure, we might even call lim friend—but sometimes it's like we have a long-distance relationship with lim. I remember an old commercial by AT&T. The tag-line was "reach out and ouch someone." AT&T had its finger on how we live: Because of college, jobs, and ountless other factors, few of us are as near as we want to be to those we love. The elephone held out the promise that we could still be close—yet of course, we all now that telephones are no replacement for real closeness.

esus offers us a close and personal relationship, but too often I seem to behave as hough we are both very busy and live far away from each other. Perhaps through rayer, I can occasionally reach out and touch Him as I do my college roommate. ut if I do, it's a long-distance prayer. The relationship Jesus wants to have with us, owever, is far from long-distance! He wants to be close—so close He can touch us.

n fact, it is out of this desire to be close that Jesus put on flesh and moved into he neighborhood.[4] He is never satisfied with the distance humans keep between hemselves and God, so He became human. He experienced what it was like to be empted in every way. He tasted suffering. He walked among us, sweated with us, nd got hungry. We can't keep him away!

t goes even deeper: Jesus wants us to be in His family, not just near Him but a part f Him in all senses. Jesus wants us to call him brother. He wants us to see Him as hough we are in His family (Matthew 12:50). And He wants the family resemblance o show. Just as a son resembles a father, so also do brothers resemble each other. rothers share bloodlines; it is for this reason we can call Jesus our brother. This is ot blasphemy. Jesus has human blood in His veins, and He wants us to see how we an be so near to Him, so in tune with His rhythms, that we look like Him more and nore. Can you see Him?

---

ohn 1:14 *The Message*

MEDITATION

▼

*Psalm 1:1-2 "Blessed is the one who does not walk in step with the wicked or stand in the way that sinners take or sit in the company of mockers, but whose delight is in the law of the Lord, and who **meditates** on his law day and night."*

The Hebrew word that is translated as "meditate" in this psalm means to growl or mutter to oneself. The picture it would elicit in the mind of an ancient Israelite is one of a lion who is enjoying his meal. He chews on the food and growls to himself in delight as he moves the choice morsels around in his mouth. This seems gruesome, but it helps us to understand what it means to meditate. It is not merely emptying your mind. It is focusing your attention in a single direction as you take delight in Scripture. Meditating on Scripture means you read a small portion and say it over and over again in your mind. You pace yourself in the Scripture and take delight in the life it brings you.

This week, meditate on the words of Matthew 3:17: "And a voice from heaven said, 'This is my son, whom I love; in whom I am well pleased." Memorize this small Scripture as an anchor for the identity of Jesus. You can also imagine God saying these words to you: This is my son/daughter, whom I love, in whom I am well pleased. Try doing this imaginative exercise for five minutes, three times today.

▼

1. What is your initial reaction to calling Jesus your brother? Why?
2. Why do you think Jesus put on flesh and became human?
3. What do you think the touch of Jesus meant to the disciples on the mountain (Matthew 17:7)?
4. In what ways does Jesus touch us and remind us that He is close?
5. How can we be more careful to notice these touches? What are the things that cause us to ignore them?

Read Matthew 17:7-8, Hebrews 4:14-16, and reflect on the week.
What has the Holy Spirit revealed to you this week?

SATURDAY | REST

*"In peace I will lie down and sleep, for
you alone, Lord, make me dwell in safety."*
Psalm 4:8

FEBRUARY - WEEK ONE

JESUS AS
MIGHTY WARRIOR

MONDAY - READ JUDGES 6-7 AND LUKE 22:42

In January, we spent some time learning to see Jesus as He truly is—the Son of God whose identity was affirmed and revealed on the mountain top, and the creator who was present in the beginning and who is still involved in making beauty out of the void in our lives. Jesus, the creator and Son of God, is near and active, and He wants to be close to us. This month, we are going to seek to see Him better by continuing our journey through the Old Testament. All Scripture points to Jesus (John 5:39), and this week, we begin in Judges with Gideon. The Jesus we meet through Gideon redefines what Israel understood as "strength" and "weakness"—and it's a lesson we still need today.

The reading for this week shows Israel in shambles. Every effort at life (planting crops, raising cattle, building homes) ends in utter destruction. The Midianites relentlessly oppress Israel, who cries out to God for help.

> " Although Gideon has his doubts, God promises to see him through to victory. "

God responds by putting together a SWAT team led by a surprising pick: Gideon. If we were selecting teams of mighty warriors, Gideon would be picked last, or maybe not at all; he is, the Scripture tells us, the "least." At the first moment we meet him, Gideon is threshing wheat by a wine press in order to hide it from the Midianites. He's being bullied—running away and hiding in fear. So when the angel who commissions Gideon calls him a "mighty warrior" and says that God is with him (v. 12), those words surely seem ironic: Gideon, a mighty man of valor? Not so much. Although Gideon has his doubts, God promises to see him through to victory, and so Gideon falls in line with the angel's invitation to get up and join God in His work.

---

*Exodus 4:22

Although there are obvious differences, there are also clear ways in which we can see Gideon as a seed of Jesus, who was born into a poor family in the middle of nowhere with no fanfare except a visit from dirty shepherds. Apparently, God likes using things that appear weak to demonstrate His strength. God likes taking those who are bullied and downtrodden and using them for His higher purposes.

This idea is also played out in how Gideon fights the Midianites. Instead of stacking Gideon's army with thousands of the most elite warriors, God whittles it down to 300 so they aren't too strong. Then He arms them not with swords or spears but with trumpets, jars, and torches—strange weapons to say the least. God used the least person in the weakest clan to lead a small troop armed with impotent weapons to defeat Israel's mightiest foe.

God's way of strength is through weakness. Gideon proves to be a "mighty warrior" not because he is strong but because the Lord is with him. When we are weak, then God can be strong in us. If Gideon is the seed of this truth, Jesus shows us what it looks like fully developed! Do you see it? Jesus is a mighty warrior who fights with surrender and love. Against these weapons there is nothing that can stand—not even death.

PRAYER

Matthew 6:9-13 - "This, then, is how you should pray: 'Our Father in heaven, hallowed be Your name, Your kingdom come, Your will be done on earth as it is in heaven. Give us this day our daily bread. And forgive our debts, as we also have forgiven our debtors. And lead us not into temptation, but deliver us from the evil one."

Prayer doesn't have to be a mystery. Jesus gives us words to pray. Have you prayed these words that Jesus commands us to pray? If not, maybe you shouldn't move on to other prayers just yet. This month, try praying the Lord's Prayer three times a day. You may have to set an alarm on your phone to remind you to do it.

▼

1. Who is the strongest person you know? Why do you consider them strong? What things come to mind when you hear the word strong?

2. The Scripture names the nations who continually resisted Israel's attempts at growth and a better life. Can you name the forces against you that seem to resist your attempts at growth (habits, laziness, wrong beliefs, relationships, spiritual warfare, etc)?

3. The nations Gideon fights are said to be stronger than Israel. What is it that gives the forces against you power over you?

4. How does surrender lead to God demonstrating His strength in us?

5. How is Luke 22:42 a demonstration of Jesus's weakness AND strength?

6. What things do you need to surrender?

....

....

....

....

....

....

....

....

....

Read Judges 6-7, Luke 22:42, and reflect on the week.
What has the Holy Spirit revealed to you this week?

▼

SATURDAY | REST

"Take my yoke upon you and learn from me, for I am gentle and humble in heart, and you will find rest for your souls."
Matthew 11:29

JESUS AS REDEEMER

MONDAY - READ RUTH 3 AND RUTH 4:13-17

We are practicing looking for Jesus in the Old Testament this month. This time we're going somewhere surprising, the book of Ruth, where the name of GOD (let alone Jesus) is not even mentioned! Bear with us, though. It may not say His name, but we'll find Jesus in a man named Boaz, who is called a "kinsman redeemer." This term points us to Jesus in ways we'll explore this week.

In Leviticus 25, we learn that If an Israelite finds himself poor and enslaved, a relative may come and purchase him out of slavery. This relative is called the "kinsman redeemer." God provided this system as a way to help His people regain freedom when they were literally enslaved, and it gives us a way to understand the process of redemption that Jesus carries out in the New Testament. Like the Old Testament kinsman redeemer, Jesus came to pay off a slave-owner to buy our freedom.

The book of Ruth shows this gracious system in action. Ruth begins her story in a bad place, with no hope for her future. She is in a foreign land with no family and no way to earn a living. Slavery is her only option...unless there is a kinsman redeemer, someone who will take her into his household, give her a future, and break the chains of slavery. To most people of her day, Ruth would be seen as a problem to be solved or a burden to bear. But Boaz loves her. To him, she is valuable and worthy of great sacrifice.

I know that I have talked to a number of Christians who need to understand this seed of Jesus better. Instead of seeing His redemptive work as an act of love that frees us from slavery to sin and makes us part of His household, we sometimes see God as an angry slave-owner who needs to be bought off. It is as though God is furious at us—even hates us and wants to destroy us—because of our sin, but Jesus steps in to save the day by offering His life. It's almost like we believe John 3:16 reads "for God so hated the world that He killed his only son." This isn't the seed of Jesus that the book of Ruth sows. Ruth paints a picture not of wrath and vengeance but of love and acceptance. The God of Ruth is not a slave-owner but a warm and welcoming husband who wants to set things right, all debts paid. He created us, so He doesn't want to destroy us; instead, He wants to build a family.

C.S. Lewis helps us understand this concept of kinsman redeemer. In The Lion, The Witch, and the Wardrobe, Aslan, a lion, is the redeemer figure, while Edmund, an adolescent boy, represents you and me. Edmund has pledged his allegiance to the White Witch, who wants to kill him and ensure that her evil reign endures. However, Aslan ends up offering his life to the White Witch so Edmund can live. The price is offered to the slave-owner and not to the creator! Many of us have found ourselves enslaved to sin and to our enemy. Because of this, we tend to believe the worst about ourselves—after all, our slave-owner is a liar and is all too quick to tell us that we are hopeless and without a future.

Perhaps you have come to believe that you are merely a problem to be solved or a burden to bear. Do you see Jesus, your kinsman redeemer, coming? To Him, you are valuable and worthy of great sacrifice.

PRAYER

▼

Matthew 6:9-13 - "This, then, is how you should pray: 'Our Father in heaven, hallowed be Your name, Your kingdom come, Your will be done on earth as it is in heaven. Give us this day our daily bread. And forgive our debts, as we also have forgiven our debtors. And lead us not into temptation, but deliver us from the evil one."

Prayer doesn't have to be a mystery. Jesus gives us words to pray. Have you prayed these words that Jesus commands us to pray? If not, maybe you shouldn't move on to other prayers just yet. This month, try praying the Lord's Prayer three times a day. You may have to set an alarm on your phone to remind you to do it.

▼

What connotation does the word "redeemer" have for you? Why?

What are some specific things that have you enslaved (habitual sins, lies of our enemy, thought patterns, etc.)?

What do you think Jesus did to redeem you from these things?

How do you receive the redemption of Jesus?

How do you think Ruth felt when Boaz proclaimed that he wanted to redeem her? When was the last time you heard Jesus proclaim His love for you? Take some time to listen for this proclamation.

Why is it significant that Ruth and Boaz's son was the grandfather of David?

....

....

....

....

....

....

....

....

....

....

Read Ruth 3, Ruth 4:13-17, and reflect on the week.
What has the Holy Spirit revealed to you this week?

▼

SATURDAY | REST

"Whenever Jesus comes he establishes rest..."
Oswald Chambers

FEBRUARY - WEEK THREE

JESUS AS FAITHFUL LOVE

MONDAY - READ HOSEA 3

Let's continue our journey of looking for Jesus in the Old Testament. Remember, all of Scripture points to Jesus—including another surprising place, the book of Hosea. This book opens with a story of a broken marriage. Hosea, the prophet, takes promiscuous Gomer as his wife. They have three children together, but then Gomer goes back to her old ways, acting out in a wildly unfaithful way. Eventually it gets so bad that Hosea has to buy her back from slavery.

We're still looking for Jesus. Remember: He is the kinsman redeemer who wants to buy us out of slavery and make us part of His family. The book of Hosea fleshes out this idea more and we are able to see how we ended up enslaved in the first place. Notice that before Gomer shows up at the slave-market, she is possessed and owned by what she loves. Her desires control her, and she has surrendered to all the wrong things. God knows the consequences of giving our hearts away, which is why He implores Israel through Hosea to remove the unfaithfulness from between [its] breasts" (Hosea 2:2). This is the reason God wants us to have no other gods beside Him and why we are instructed to love Him with all of our heart, soul, mind, and strength. When we love other things, we give those things the power to rule us. Those other rulers will ravage you and leave you harassed and helpless. Not only does sin hurt the heart of God, but it hurts us as well. Indeed, the wages of sin is death.

Now we're ready to see Jesus. Gomer's adultery is not the only thing highlighted in this story. While it understandably hurts and angers Hosea that his wife repeatedly takes other lovers, he can't turn his back on her and he literally buys her back from the slave market. In a striking contrast to Gomer's unfaithfulness, Hosea's faithful love shines through. In the same way, as we come to understand how our sins hurt and anger God, we can see more clearly the faithful love of Jesus who is willing, like Hosea, to buy us back from lesser things that have captured our hearts. When those other things ultimately fail us, Jesus is there to "allure" us and "speak tenderly" to us (Hosea 2:14). He wants to win our hearts back!

PRAYER

Matthew 6:9-13 - "This, then, is how you should pray: 'Our Father in heaven, hallowed be Your name, Your kingdom come, Your will be done on earth as it is in heaven. Give us this day our daily bread. And forgive our debts, as we also have forgiven our debtors. And lead us not into temptation, but deliver us from the evil one."

Prayer doesn't have to be a mystery. Jesus gives us words to pray. Have you prayed these words that Jesus commands us to pray? If not, maybe you shouldn't move on to other prayers just yet. This month, try praying the Lord's Prayer three times a day. You may have to set an alarm on your phone to remind you to do it.

1. What do we learn about the character of Jesus by looking at how Hosea treated Gomer? In what ways are you like Gomer?

2. How does idolatry relate to adultery?

3. How do you see this truth played out in your life? How have you become owned by what you love?

4. What do you think it means for God to "speak tenderly" to you in the wilderness (Hosea 2:14)? Have you ever heard this tender voice of God? Describe it.

5. Can you name your other lovers? How do you think God feels about those other loves?

6. What is one thing you can do this week to turn from a lesser love toward Jesus?

Read Hosea 3 and reflect on the week.
What has the Holy Spirit revealed to you this week?

SATURDAY | REST

*"You will keep in perfect peace those whose
minds are steadfast, because they trust in you."*
Isaiah 26:3

FEBRUARY - WEEK FOUR

JESUS AS OUR DELIVERER

MONDAY - READ DANIEL 3

Usually when people say, "Deliver me," they mean something like, "GET ME OUT OF THIS!" or "RESCUE ME!" So to call Jesus our deliverer means we are calling Him our rescuer. That is who He is. But He often doesn't deliver in the ways we wish He would. This week's Scripture, Daniel 3, points to Jesus just as Ruth and Hosea did, and just like these other passages, it shows us that sometimes He shows up in ways we don't expect.

In this passage, we learn that there is an evil plot and a terrible command that threatens God's people. The Jews in this story have to choose between worshipping the king and worshipping their God; they are directly in the crosshairs of a culture war, and their allegiance to God is going to cost them. We will all face moments like this in which we know that we are going to be thrown into the fire. It may not be a literal fire, but we will suffer as the force of the culture comes against us. Where is Jesus in moments like these?

Personally, I would prefer to be delivered from the fire by not having to face it at all. I want Jesus to deliver me by plucking me out of whatever fire I'm in, or maybe by removing the fire itself and leaving me right where I am. I imagine that Shadrach, Meshach, and Abednego might have hoped or prayed that God would put out the flames with a mighty wind or snuff them with His hand—or perhaps they hoped He would whisk them away to somewhere safe. He answers their prayers for deliverance, though, by getting into the fire with them. This is an extremely personal way to deliver.

We read that Shadrach, Meshach, and Abednego are walking around in the fire with the Son of Man. In Bible lingo, the phrase "walking with God" means that someone has a conversational relationship with God. Enoch walks with God. Noah walks with God. Here, Shadrach, Meshach, and Abednego are walking with God—literally.

I'll bet if you could ask Shadrach, Meshach, and Abednego if they wished God had removed them from the flames, they would have to admit that they had the better experience: "Why would we take away the fire and miss a chance to walk with Jesus?!"

Maybe you're in the fire right now. The fire is a good place to look for Jesus. I'm confident He's in there with you, and I trust that this fire will help you to draw closer to God and experience His nearness in ways you just couldn't experience otherwise.

PRAYER

▼

Matthew 6:9-13 - "This, then, is how you should pray: 'Our Father in heaven, hallowed be Your name, Your kingdom come, Your will be done on earth as it is in heaven. Give us this day our daily bread. And forgive our debts, as we also have forgiven our debtors. And lead us not into temptation, but deliver us from the evil one.'"

Prayer doesn't have to be a mystery. Jesus gives us words to pray. Have you prayed these words that Jesus commands us to pray? If not, maybe you shouldn't move on to other prayers just yet. This month, try praying the Lord's Prayer three times a day. You may have to set an alarm on your phone to remind you to do it.

▼

Think of a time in your life when you were "in the flames." Now look for Jesus. Where was He? What was He doing? What did He say?

Do you believe all the "fire" you experience in life comes from God? Where did the fire that Shadrach, Meshach, and Abednego experienced come from?

How can God use other people to demonstrate His presence in the midst of our fire?

What does it mean to get into other people's fire? Is this something Christians should do? Why do we avoid this?

....

....

....

....

....

....

....

....

....

....

....

Read Daniel 3 and reflect on the week.
What has the Holy Spirit revealed to you this week?

SATURDAY | REST

"Therefore, since the promise of entering his rest still stands, let us be careful that none of you be found to have fallen short of it." Hebrews 4:1

MARCH - WEEK ONE

JESUS AS THE LAMB

MONDAY - READ 1 PETER 1:18-21 AND REVELATION 5

During the past two months, we have practiced seeing Jesus more clearly by meditating on various facets of His identity (January) and by learning to read familiar Old Testament stories through new eyes, as seeds that God plants to prepare the way for Jesus's coming. When Jesus does come, it is not as a triumphant, conquering military hero but as a suffering servant whose main redemptive purpose is achieved through sacrifice. This month, we will focus on the idea of sacrifice and exploring it through both the Old and New Testaments will help us to see Jesus more clearly.

Sacrifice plays a key role in one of the most pivotal stories in the history of the Jewish people: the Exodus from Egypt. At this point in the story, Moses has approached Pharoah and asked for release from slavery. So far, nine plagues have devastated Egypt yet still the Jewish people are enslaved. But then God tells His people to reserve a lamb "without defect" to sacrifice. They are to eat this lamb and paint its blood on their doorways, a visible sign of their participation in God's plan. Sure, it's gruesome. But they know that it is the blood of this lamb that will protect them as they are ushered out of slavery and into the promises of God.

> " When Jesus does come, it is not as a triumphant, conquering military hero but as a suffering servant whose main redemptive purpose is achieved through sacrifice. "

To the Jew, the sacrifice of the lamb is the first chapter in the story of Israel's becoming God's people. Their identity is further fleshed out when God gives these people ten commandments and a book of laws to distinguish them from the other nations of the world. It is solidified on Mt. Sinai when God tells them He is choosing them as a kingdom of priests—a holy nation (Exodus 19). God reminds His people that they are to be like that lamb—unblemished—and that in a life of purity and holiness, freedom from bondage can be found.

Yet over and over again, Israel chooses wrongly and is covered in the dirt of sin. They simply cannot live up to the identity God has in mind for them. These people need a new lamb.

Peter thus describes Jesus as this new lamb "without blemish or defect." Through His sacrifice, He buys His people from the enemy that owns them and provides a new Exodus, not away from Egypt but away from sin and death. The seeds of Jesus in the Old Testament have sprouted, as again there is a Lamb that sets people free and calls them to a vocation in the world.

In Revelation 5, John sees this story from yet another angle—heaven! John sees a scroll that contains God's desire for creation, but there is no one who can open it, and there is great mourning. If no one can open the scroll, how will God's kingdom ever come? Just when things seem utterly hopeless, along comes a lamb who is able to open the scroll. He is worthy and makes for Himself a kingdom of priests and a holy nation (vs. 10). We are told that this lamb is the center-focus of all of heaven. When He opens the scroll, all of heaven erupts in worship. I think this should be our response as well when we see Jesus as the Lamb!

FASTING

▼

Matthew 6:16-18 - "When you fast, do not look somber as the hypocrites do, for they disfigure their faces to show others they are fasting. Truly I tell you, they have received their reward in full. But when you fast, put oil on your head and wash your face, so that it will not be obvious to others that you are fasting, but only to your Father, who is unseen; and your Father, who sees what is done in secret, will reward you."

Job 23:12 - "I have not departed from the commands of his lips; I have treasured the words of his mouth more than my daily bread."

Jesus gives us guidance on how to fast because He assumes we will fast. This is not a super-spiritual discipline meant for the elite. It is a normal Christian activity meant for all the disciples of Jesus. Fasting is simply denying immediate appetites so we can focus on eternal ones. Try fasting all day today. As you get hungry, simply direct your attention to God and repeat the words of Job, "I treasure your Words more than my daily bread."

1. In the story of Israel's Exodus, the lamb is not the end. It is the beginning. How is Jesus setting you free from sin the beginning of your Christian story rather than the end? Does this change your perspective of the Christian life? How so?

2. When the lamb sets people free, it is for a reason: they are set free to accomplish something. What does God free Israel to do in the world? What does Jesus free you to do in the world?

3. How is Jesus able to "open the scroll" thereby opening up God's desire for creation? How do you think the scroll got locked in the first place?

4. In what ways do you worship Jesus for being the Lamb who set you free and opened God's will for your life?

Read 1 Peter 1:18-21, Revelation 5, and reflect on the week.

What has the Holy Spirit revealed to you this week?

SATURDAY | REST

"The Lord is my shepherd, I lack nothing. He makes me lie down in green pastures, he leads me beside quiet waters, he refreshes my soul."

Psalm 23:1-3

MARCH - WEEK TWO

JESUS as THE OFFERING

MONDAY - READ LEVITICUS 1:1-2 AND HEBREWS 10:1-14

Wait, God doesn't want sacrifice? Isn't that the point of the whole book of Leviticus?

This scripture ought to make us stop and think because it's revolutionary. More specifically, the first two verses of Leviticus are revolutionary because they establish that God is personal and wants people to draw close to Him. How do we see this more clearly? First, let's talk about the word "YHWH." This is God's personal name revealed to Israel. Whenever a Biblical author wants to enact the covenant or get people to think about God in personal ways, he uses this word. He's not just any old god going about His business and not caring about people: He's Yahweh!

Furthermore, let's unpack what's going on when God declares to Moses what should happen "when anyone brings an offering." Isn't this just a command to donate to the work of the Lord? Maybe it's partly that, but it's also much more. The root word for the word that we translate "offering" contains within it an idea that matters greatly here: to "come close or come near." To bring an offering is to come near. Right off the bat, then, this book speaks of a God who has come close to a group of people and invites (even expects) them to come close to Him! The sacrifice was meant to ease the conscience of the people so they could come close to God—YHWH.

Yet God wants so much more for us than to come near occasionally when we bring a gift to Him. He wants us to obey fully, to offer ourselves as true sacrifices, as that is the path to true closeness. God isn't after sacrifice; He's after nearness. Therefore, obedience is better than sacrifice. As the author of Hebrews reminds us, sacrifices offered year after year won't work, as they do nothing to make perfect those who draw near to worship. In fact, they just remind us of our sins! The writer of Hebrews quotes Psalm 40, which presents a better way—a body for perfect obedience rather than a sacrifice for disobedience. Jesus was this offering of perfect obedience.

As we know already, we can't obey perfectly on our own. But look at Jesus. He's the offering that makes a way for us to be "made holy." By His offering, we are now able to offer ourselves as living sacrifices, holy and pleasing to the Lord. This offering touches every facet of our lives: finances, relationships, vocation, education, the words we speak, the people we befriend, the movies we watch, etc. There is nothing in our lives that this offering does not transform into an act of obedience. Jesus demonstrates for us the path of making an offering out of our whole lives. This is how we draw close to God. Do you see it?

---

²Exodus 4:22

FASTING

▼

Matthew 6:16-18 - "When you fast, do not look somber as the hypocrites do, for they disfigure their faces to show others they are fasting. Truly I tell you, they have received their reward in full. But when you fast, put oil on your head and wash your face, so that it will not be obvious to others that you are fasting, but only to your Father, who is unseen; and your Father, who sees what is done in secret, will reward you."

Job 23:12 - "I have not departed from the commands of his lips; I have treasured the words of his mouth more than my daily bread."

Jesus gives us guidance on how to fast because He assumes we will fast. This is not a super-spiritual discipline meant for the elite. It is a normal Christian activity meant for all the disciples of Jesus. Fasting is simply denying immediate appetites so we can focus on eternal ones. Try fasting all day today. As you get hungry, simply direct your attention to God and repeat the words of Job, "I treasure your Words more than my daily bread."

1. What is your response to hearing that God has never wanted or needed sacrifice?
2. Why do you think God wants obedience rather than sacrifice?
3. To what does the obedience of Jesus open the door in our relationship with God?
4. What in your life has not been offered to God?
5. What might perfect obedience look like for you right now? Is there some specific way in which God is asking you to obey Him? What is it?

Read Leviticus 1:1-2, Hebrews 10:1-14, and reflect on the week.
What has the Holy Spirit revealed to you this week?

SATURDAY | REST

"I said, 'Oh, that I had the wings of a dove! I would fly away and be at rest.'" Psalm 55:6

MARCH - WEEK THREE

JESUS AS SUFFERING SERVANT

MONDAY - READ JOHN 11:1-37 AND ISAIAH 53:4-6

In the past two weeks, we have seen the sacrifice Jesus made with His death to purchase our freedom from slavery and the offering up of His whole life in perfect obedience. Now, we see the sacrifice that He makes in becoming human and sharing our brokenness. How do we know it was a sacrifice for Him? Because Jesus wept. It's the shortest verse in the Bible, but it says so much. Becoming human cost Him dearly—but it also allows Him to share our feelings, to suffer with us. Sometimes we think that God sits high above everything and is unmoved by the suffering we experience. We say things like "God is still on the throne" or "everything happens for a reason." Those are well-intentioned phrases and may be fine things to say. But we are missing something of Jesus's character if we think that He is unmoved by our hurt.

Why does He weep at Lazarus's death? Remember, Jesus was present when the earth was formed. He knows what it was meant to be. He was there when humanity was made and God said it was "very good." Imagine how it must have felt for him to walk through this world He made and see sickness, disease, oppression, drought, and all the other things that mar its beauty. The fact that Jesus knows what creation could be and should be only amplifies the depth of His pain at seeing it broken. And so He weeps. Jesus is God who enters into our pain and cries with us. He is not unmoved. He suffers with us.

When Jesus weeps, some in the story are struck by the depth of His compassion: "See how much He loved," they say. But others doubt His power—if He is really God, why doesn't He just make the pain go away? Isn't that the age-old question? If God is powerful enough to heal and loving enough to care, why is there so much suffering? Jesus demonstrates that God's answer to suffering isn't to eradicate it but to go all the way in and all the way down.

Why is this? Because the evil in the world that causes so much suffering isn't only "out there." It's also in us. So if Jesus is going to heal the world's suffering, He has to work from the inside out, getting inside humanity and bearing the suffering in Himself. In fact, this is foretold in Isaiah 53:4-6. Jesus bears our griefs, carries our sorrows, takes the bruises that should have been ours. He climbs in the fire with us—and in so doing, He delivers us, heals us, and sets a path toward restoring the whole world.

Do you see Him now? The great suffering servant who is willing to bear the suffering of the world?

FASTING

▼

Matthew 6:16-18 - "When you fast, do not look somber as the hypocrites do, for they disfigure their faces to show others they are fasting. Truly I tell you, they have received their reward in full. But when you fast, put oil on your head and wash your face, so that it will not be obvious to others that you are fasting, but only to your Father, who is unseen; and your Father, who sees what is done in secret, will reward you."

Job 23:12 - "I have not departed from the commands of his lips; I have treasured the words of his mouth more than my daily bread."

Jesus gives us guidance on how to fast because He assumes we will fast. This is not a super-spiritual discipline meant for the elite. It is a normal Christian activity meant for all the disciples of Jesus. Fasting is simply denying immediate appetites so we can focus on eternal ones. Try fasting all day today. As you get hungry, simply direct your attention to God and repeat the words of Job, "I treasure your Words more than my daily bread."

▼

1. Can you testify to an instance in which you saw the faithfulness of God's presence in the midst of your suffering? What did His presence mean to you in that moment?

2. Do you believe Jesus actually hurts with us? Does this comfort you? Why/Why not?

3. How does Jesus entering into suffering help heal the world's suffering? How does it heal your own suffering when Jesus enters it with you?

4. In the Lazarus story, Jesus also points to resurrection, which is a whole new creation. How does hope in a new creation help people move forward in the midst of suffering?

Read John 11:1-37, Isaiah 53:4-6, and reflect on the week.
What has the Holy Spirit revealed to you this week?

SATURDAY | REST

*Peace I leave with you; my peace I give you. I
do not give to you as the world gives. Do not let
your hearts be troubled and do not be afraid.*

John 14:27

MARCH - WEEK FOUR

JESUS AS OUR PEACE

MONDAY - READ COLOSSIANS 1:15-23

The Jewish people use the word "Shalom" for "peace." While that word does mean peace, there's a depth to it that we might miss if we're not careful. We need to understand the fuller meaning of Shalom if we're to understand what it means to see Jesus as our peace.

Genesis 1 and 2 paint a picture of a united creation. People have an unbroken relationship with God, with creation, and with each other. This shadow of complete union and intimacy still haunts us (in a good way), like a dream we can't quite capture but also can't help but chase. We live in a post-Genesis 3 world, with the effects of Adam and Eve's fall all around us, but we long for our relationship with the earth, with each other, and with our creator to be restored. Instead, we struggle as the earth fights back at us with thorns, wild animals, earthquakes, and floods. We fight each other in wars, oppression, and divorce. We line up as enemies of God with our sin and rebellion. Yet with every alarm bell that something is not right, we are reminded of what could be. We long to be made whole again.

This is what Shalom means: one-ness or unity. Peace by this definition isn't an absence of conflict or a negotiated cease-fire but rather a sort of systemic harmony, where everything works together toward growth, life, and balance.

With that in mind, we read Paul's words to the Colossians in new light. We were enemies of God in our own minds. The relationship was broken because of our evil behavior. But God has reconciled us through Jesus's blood to make peace, that is, to restore a broken relationship to wholeness. This is what atonement means. If we break up the word, it means at-one-ment. We were once "at one" with God, creation, and each other. All of those relationships have been broken. But Jesus makes us at-one again.

Perhaps you desperately want to experience this kind of peace but you feel like it is always just out of reach. You hear the promise, but you can't seem to feel the oneness. This can happen when we have competing desires in our hearts. We may want to be united with God but we also want to make money, eat well, live comfortably, etc. The offer of peace is also an offer to make Jesus your number one desire. It is a call to let everything else go.

Can we be at one with creation without the intercession of Jesus? Is it possible to truly be at one with your spouse apart from the work of Christ? What about being reconciled to God? There is one path to being made whole, and that is Jesus Christ. Can you see Jesus as this atonement (at-one-ment)?

FASTING

▼

Matthew 6:16-18 - "When you fast, do not look somber as the hypocrites do, for they disfigure their faces to show others they are fasting. Truly I tell you, they have received their reward in full. But when you fast, put oil on your head and wash your face, so that it will not be obvious to others that you are fasting, but only to your Father, who is unseen; and your Father, who sees what is done in secret, will reward you."

Job 23:12 - "I have not departed from the commands of his lips; I have treasured the words of his mouth more than my daily bread."

Jesus gives us guidance on how to fast because He assumes we will fast. This is not a super-spiritual discipline meant for the elite. It is a normal Christian activity meant for all the disciples of Jesus. Fasting is simply denying immediate appetites so we can focus on eternal ones. Try fasting all day today. As you get hungry, simply direct your attention to God and repeat the words of Job, "I treasure your Words more than my daily bread."

▼

1. How would you define the word "peace"?
2. How does the Jewish understanding of Shalom (peace) change your understanding of what peace is?
3. What does Paul mean when he says we were once alienated from God and enemies in our minds?
4. What does Paul mean when he says Jesus made "peace through his blood shed on a cross?"
5. Do you feel at peace with God? Why/why not?

....

....

....

....

....

....

....

....

....

....

....

....

....

Read Colossians 1:15-23 and reflect on the week.
What has the Holy Spirit revealed to you this week?

SATURDAY | REST

"There remains, then, a Sabbath-rest for the people of God; for anyone who enters God's rest also rests from their works, just as God did from his."
Hebrews 4:9-10

APRIL - WEEK ONE

JESUS AS CHAMPION

MONDAY - READ ZECHARIAH 9:9-10 AND MARK 11:1-10

We are kicking off another approach to Jesus during these next three months—Living Him. We have learned to see Him more clearly already, and that process culminated in a discussion of the ways that His sacrifice brings us Shalom, the peace that comes with living in full harmony with God. Today's Scriptures show us one way that those who are in harmony with God live differently—specifically, where they place their confidence and hope.

Some biblical scholars believe there were two processions heading into Jerusalem on Palm Sunday. These represent two different approaches to this question of hope. Jesus enters the holy city from the east, riding on a donkey. By contrast, with his imperial cavalry and soldiers in attendance, Governor Pilate arrives majestically from the west. The two processions are entering the city for different purposes: Jesus as the Prince of Peace and Pilate as a keeper of the peace. Two powers are coming to face each other in Jerusalem's center ring. Which champion will win?

A lot is at stake for Pilate in this scene. This is a volatile time, and Pilate has been assigned to Jerusalem to keep the peace and make sure there is no uprising during an important religious festival. There have been a number of uprisings before this day, and the Roman overseers have been removed because of them. Pilate's goal is to display Rome's military might, mostly in order to dissuade any other Jews who might attempt to drive out Roman occupation. Pilate's procession is surely grand, with legions of armed soldiers awing those attending into submission to Caesar. Most of the people who lined the streets recognize its purpose: a raw display of military intimidation.

Jesus comes into Jerusalem from a different direction. There is no demonstration of force or display of power. In fact, He comes in riding a donkey. His people wave palm branches instead of swords and shout, "Hosanna, blessed is He who comes in the name of the Lord" rather than hailing the name of Caesar.

Jerusalem on Palm Sunday, then, can be seen as the story of two champions: the champion of Rome sent to keep the peace (by force) and the champion of Heaven sent to bring peace (by sacrifice). Both champions (Pilate and Jesus) have come to fight an enemy. Pilate comes to fight a possible insurgency, and he does it with the usual means: soldiers, weapons, and intimidation. But Jesus comes to fight a different power, and to do that, He has to be a new kind of champion, one whose power was not in military strength but in His love and self-sacrifice. Jesus will prove to be strong enough to overthrow not only the Roman government but also the law of sin and death.

This begs a question. Which champion are you betting on?

We bet with our lives. Pilate asks us to accumulate wealth, political power, and influence. Jesus asks us to give ourselves away. My feeling is that we say with our mouths that Jesus is our champion and yet too often we bet with our lives on the way of Pilate. Lord have mercy.

CELEBRATION

▼

Richard Foster claims that "Celebration is at the heart of the way of Christ."[18] He explains by highlighting the fact that Jesus entered the world with jubilant angels announcing "good news of great joy!" Then, as He was departing the world, Jesus passes down His joy to his disciples: "These things I have spoken to you that my joy may be in you, and that your joy may be full."

One way to celebrate is to clap and make noise. Today, while you're stopped at a traffic light, try applauding all that God has done in your life. You can clap and shout and lift your hands.

[18] Richard Foster, *Celebration of Discipline* (New York, NY: HarperSanFransisco, 1998); 190.

▼

1. Why do you think Jesus chose to enter Jerusalem on a donkey?

2. What is the crowd waving palm branches expecting from Jesus? What might the same crowd be expecting from Pilate?

3. Which champion are you betting your life on (Pilate or Jesus)? How so?

....

....

....

....

....

....

....

....

....

....

....

....

....

....

Read Zechariah 9:9-10, Mark 11:1-10, and reflect on the week.
What has the Holy Spirit revealed to you this week?

SATURDAY | REST

*"In repentance and rest is your salvation, in quietness
and trust is your strength..." Isaiah 30:15*

APRIL - WEEK TWO

JESUS AS THE GARDNER

MONDAY - READ JOHN 19:41-42 AND JOHN 20:11-18

She thought he was the gardener! Talk about a loaded phrase!

For the Jewish people, the whole story begins in a garden. The first thing we see God doing in Genesis 2 is playing in the dirt to make humans. Then God places humanity within a garden He makes. Humans are given extreme creative power and responsibility to cultivate the garden. As we have discussed (and as we all know simply from paying attention to the brokenness around us), humans use their freedom to bring sin and destruction into God's creation. We are still feeling the effects of that today. So when Jesus, our champion and our hope, re-emerges into the world He made, it makes sense that He does so in a garden.

This time, the story is not about the destruction of a beautiful, harmonious world, but of resurrection. Let's go to the garden where John places us. It's nothing like Eden. Eden was fresh and new, but John's garden is old, and it has seen many people die. Creation is worn out, busted up. But in the midst of it, there's a new tomb. No one has been laid in a tomb like this. This was a unique death. Out of this new tomb comes the resurrection and the life. There it is: new creation bursting forth right in the middle of the old. Think about it. Jesus is buried in the earth and then He rises. What happens in a garden? Seeds are buried underneath soil. They have to die and rise out of that same soil. When they do, they provide life and food for all of creation.

Resurrection—living Jesus—is not about escaping from the world but rather participating in the new creation that is breaking forth. We can see its fruits in how we approach our marriages, our friendships, how we plant a garden, raise our children, sell insurance, buy a car, go to school, craft furniture, read a book, create antidotes to viruses...resurrection brings new life to an old world like new buds bring life to an old garden. And Jesus is the gardener who is bringing these buds into bloom.   No wonder Mary thought He was the gardener.

CELEBRATION

▼

Richard Foster claims that "Celebration is at the heart of the way of Christ."[18] He explains by highlighting the fact that Jesus entered the world with jubilant angels announcing "good news of great joy!" Then, as He was departing the world, Jesus passes down His joy to his disciples: "These things I have spoken to you that my joy may be in you, and that your joy may be full."

One way to celebrate is to clap and make noise. Today, while you're stopped at a traffic light, try applauding all that God has done in your life. You can clap and shout and lift your hands.

[18] Richard Foster, *Celebration of Discipline* (New York, NY: HarperSanFransisco, 1998); 190.

1. If Jesus is the gardener that brings new life in the midst of an old creation, what does it mean for Him to "weed" your life?
2. Where are you seeing new life bursting forth right now?
3. Where are you seeing the need to plant some seeds of new life? How do you do that?

Read John 19:41-42, John 20:11-18, and reflect on the week.
What has the Holy Spirit revealed to you this week?

▼

SATURDAY | REST

"Be still before the LORD and wait patiently for him"
Psalm 37:7a

JESUS AS OUR HOPE

MONDAY - READ 1 CORINTHIANS 15:12-28

In the beginning, God's space and our space were united. We enjoyed unbroken fellowship with God, each other, and creation. Through our own disobedience, we drove God out of our own space and created a world in which we, not God, decided what was good and evil. We wanted to be the masters of our world. However, we proved to be terrible masters, ushering in death, torture, decay, and brokenness. It's enough to make us want to run away—and in fact many people think that our main Christian hope is to one day leave this earth that we've destroyed and go live in God's space (heaven) forever. That may fill us with some comfort. But that is not the final hope of a follower of Jesus. God wants more for us than escape; He wants to remake the world with us.

Jesus demonstrates what it looks like to live in union with God. His resurrection is the proof that His way of living is more powerful than death—that it is indeed the way of eternal life. Our hope is that God will remake everything and that we will enjoy full fellowship with Him again. When Paul calls the resurrection of Jesus the first fruit of a new creation, he is saying that the new creation has already begun in Jesus. This is why we have hope in its coming; it has already started to bloom! The declaration "Jesus is alive" is our hope that this old creation isn't the last one. It is the hope-filled promise that sin and death do not have the final word.

One day, God's space and our space will be united again. There will be no more death. God will dry our tears. We will be His people, and He will be our God. One day, this old creation will be remade. This hope should impact the way we live. Are we living in an old creation that will pass away or anticipating a new creation that is coming? Are we living Jesus?

CELEBRATION

▼

Richard Foster claims that "Celebration is at the heart of the way of Christ."[18] He explains by highlighting the fact that Jesus entered the world with jubilant angels announcing "good news of great joy!"   Then, as He was departing the world, Jesus passes down His joy to his disciples: "These things I have spoken to you that my joy may be in you, and that your joy may be full."

One way to celebrate is to clap and make noise. Today, while you're stopped at a traffic light, try applauding all that God has done in your life. You can clap and shout and lift your hands.

[18] *Richard Foster, Celebration of Discipline (New York, NY: HarperSanFransisco, 1998); 190.*

▼

.   Why do you think many Christians believe "going to heaven when they die" is the main Christian hope? Do you think that is an incomplete hope? Why/Why not?

2. If resurrection and new creation is our final hope, what changes in the way we live and share the Gospel?

3. How might someone living under oppression or abuse be comforted by the hope of new creation?

4. How is the Holy Spirit a deposit of our hope?

5. What did Paul mean by the phrase, "Christ in you, the hope of glory?"

....

....

....

....

....

....

....

....

....

....

....

....

Read 1 Corinthians 15:12-28 and reflect on the week.
What has the Holy Spirit revealed to you this week?

SATURDAY | REST

*"Wait for the Lord; be strong and take
heart and wait for the Lord."*
Psalm 27:14

JESUS AS THE TREASURE

MONDAY - READ MATTHEW 13:44-46 AND MATTHEW 16:24-27

They say you get what you pay for. My son used to love buying vending machine toys. They were only a quarter! But they would inevitably break after a few minutes, leaving him without a toy AND without his quarter. While we love cheap things, they usually don't work the way we want them to. I'm afraid we have come to see Jesus's offer of free salvation as what Bonhoeffer calls "cheap grace."[5] It costs us nothing and, well, we get what we pay for. Jesus says some difficult things in this week's portion of Scripture. But it only feels difficult because many of us are more accustomed to seeing the benefits of following Jesus without the cost. This week, we will focus on the cost—but it is in counting the cost that the hope Jesus offers moves more sharply into focus.

As we approach this Scripture, we need to recall that it was an honor to be invited to follow a rabbi as a disciple. It meant the rabbi believed you could be like him; he saw potential in you. The whole trajectory of the education system in Jesus's day was toward becoming a rabbi. As children, Jewish boys would study the Torah. Only the brightest and most talented were invited to be a disciple of a rabbi. Here, Jesus sets the invitation in front of a group of ordinary men who have already flunked out and ended up fishing instead. This is their chance to go back to school—to reach that goal they thought they had missed. No wonder they jump at it.

The same invitation is set before us. You don't have to be seen as "good enough" to accept this invitation; you can be a common fisherman! The disciples don't have any illusions that studying with Jesus will be easy or cheap, and we shouldn't either. Quite on the contrary, the cost of being Jesus's disciple is very clear. Everything. But because they want to save their lives, they're willing to lose it all.

Jesus gets at this truth by telling a story of a man who found a treasure in a field. With joy, the man sells all he has to buy the field. He is willing to sell everything because he values the treasure more than everything else he owned. This is what Jesus is getting at. The cost of following Jesus, of living Jesus, is steep—your whole life—but what you receive is worth more than what you give up. It is totally worth it.

Dietrich Bonhoeffer. *The Cost of Discipleship* (New York, NY:Touchstone, 1995); 43.

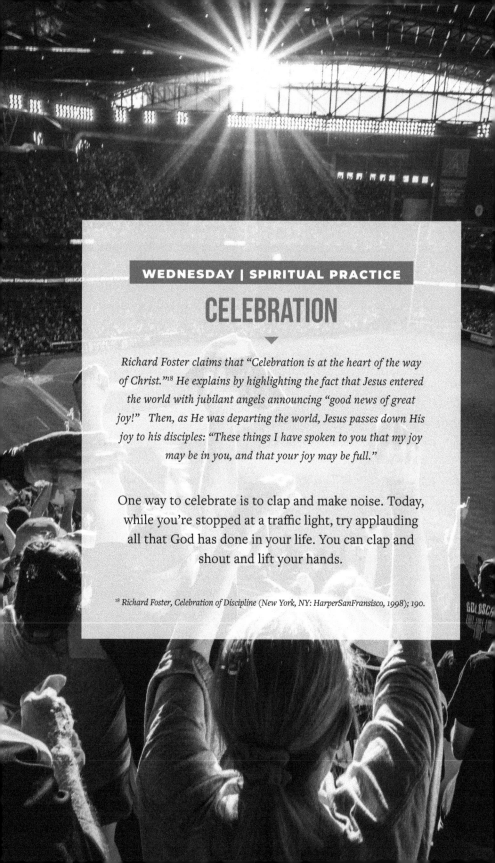

CELEBRATION

▼

Richard Foster claims that "Celebration is at the heart of the way of Christ."[18] He explains by highlighting the fact that Jesus entered the world with jubilant angels announcing "good news of great joy!" Then, as He was departing the world, Jesus passes down His joy to his disciples: "These things I have spoken to you that my joy may be in you, and that your joy may be full."

One way to celebrate is to clap and make noise. Today, while you're stopped at a traffic light, try applauding all that God has done in your life. You can clap and shout and lift your hands.

[18] Richard Foster, *Celebration of Discipline* (New York, NY: HarperSanFransisco, 1998); 190.

1. What do you think Dietrich Bonhoeffer means by the term "cheap grace"?

2. Is it possible to be a disciple of Jesus without giving Him everything? How so?

3. What does it mean to give Jesus everything? How do you do this?

4. Is there something in your life now that you are holding on to? What is it?

5. What would it look like to surrender that thing to Jesus?

Read Matthew 13:44-46, Matthew 16:24-27, and reflect on the week.
What has the Holy Spirit revealed to you this week?

SATURDAY | REST

"...but those who hope in the Lord will renew their strength. They will soar on wings like eagles; they will run and not grow weary, they will walk and not be faint."
Isaiah 40:31

MAY · WEEK ONE

JESUS AS THE WAY

MONDAY - MATTHEW 11:27-30 AND JOHN 14:5-7

As we seek to live Jesus, we have to be willing to take a risk on Him—to give up everything, to put our full confidence in Him and Him only, without keeping back anything or investing elsewhere just to hedge our bets. Understandably, this might make us nervous. It's a big risk! No wonder Thomas wanted Jesus to show him just how the process would go. "Show us the way," Thomas says, and can't we all identify?

But Jesus offers another way to understand what this journey with Him looks like. Instead of living by a map, we must put on a yoke. What is a yoke? It's what we're hooked to, or what goes with us wherever we go. Everyone is yoked to something—shame, guilt, work, money, pleasure, etc. We weren't made for those yokes, and they will wear us out. Instead, we were made to be united with God in perfect peace and harmony (Shalom). Jesus's invitation is to throw off the old yokes and become yoked together with Him.

Some believe that the whole point of Christianity is to simply believe that Jesus died for our sins so we are forgiven and go to heaven when we die. But this is nowhere in the message of Jesus or the New Testament. Why—if all we need to worry about is having our belief system in order—does Jesus say to "take my yoke upon yourself and learn from me?" This implies a whole way of life, not just a belief that we are forgiven.

Some years ago A. W. Tozer expressed his concern that "a notable heresy has come into being throughout evangelical Christian circles—the widely-accepted concept that we humans can choose to accept Christ only because we need him as Savior and that we have the right to postpone our obedience to him as Lord as long as we want to!"[6] He then goes on to state "that salvation apart from obedience is unknown in the sacred scriptures."

When you stop to think about it, why would anyone trust Jesus for something big like opening the gates of heaven when they die without also trusting that He knows how you should live before that day? If He was right about how to find forgiveness, then why not also say He was right about everything else?

---

[6] A.W. Tozer, *I Call It Heresy* (Harrisburg, PA: Christian Publications, 1974); 5f

If we really believe that Jesus knows the way, then we will naturally want to stay as close to Him as possible. We will want to hear what He has to say about our jobs, relationships, and habits. Staying close to Jesus looks a lot like being yoked to Him.

> " Come to me, all you who are weary and burdened, and I will give you rest. "

Jesus offers a yoke rather than a map because the way to intimacy with God and life to the full is by staying as close to Jesus as you can, following Him step by step in every aspect of your life.

Hear the invitation anew: "Come to me, all you who are weary and burdened, and I will give you rest. Take my yoke upon you and learn from me, for I am gentle and humble in heart, and you will find rest for your souls. For my yoke is easy and my burden is light."

SERVICE

Mark 10:45 - "For even the Son of Man did not come to be served, but to serve, and to give his life as a ransom for many."

Service is simply putting someone else's needs above your own. It can be a large or a small gesture. It certainly doesn't have to be complicated. Look for a tangible way to serve someone today and then do it.

▼

1. What do you think it means to want a "map" for Christianity?

2. What does it mean to approach Scripture as if we are looking for a map?

3. Jesus doesn't offer a map, He offers a yoke. How are these different?

4. How do you take the yoke of Jesus on you?

5. What is your response to A.W. Tozer's statement, "...salvation apart from obedience is unknown in the sacred scriptures"?

Read Matthew 11:27-30 and John 14:5-7, and reflect on the week.
What has the Holy Spirit revealed to you this week?

SATURDAY | REST

"Be still before the Lord and wait patiently for him..."
Psalm 37:7

MAY - WEEK TWO

JESUS THE INVITATION TO WALK IN THE WAY

MONDAY - READ JOHN 14:5-7 AND MATTHEW 11:27-30

Last week, we explored the idea that the way is not a list of ideas or beliefs. Rather, it is a person—the person of Jesus. If we want to know the way to live life to the full, we must be yoked with Jesus. Jesus's invitation, however, is not ONLY to take His yoke. That is the first step. We also have to surrender all the other things to which we are yoked. Then, Jesus tells us to learn from Him. This is the way of Jesus.

I never got around to training my dog very well. With children and work and T.V. watching, there just seemed to be no time! So when we go for a walk, I have to have her on a leash. She darts around me to the right and then quickly cuts to the left, jerking my arm with every movement. Then she stretches at the leash in an attempt to run forward. Next, she'll be sniffing something and I'll have to pull her to match my stride. It's true that my dog is "yoked" to me. But she has yet to learn from me. I'm guessing that she sees the leash only as something that keeps her from doing what she wants to do. However, I have her on a leash because I know the way around the neighborhood and how to get her safely back to our house. I know the danger of vehicles, other dogs, and snakes. I am not trying to imprison her with my leash. I am trying to save her life! At some point, we have not only to take on the yoke of Jesus, but also to learn how to walk with Him. After all, He's not trying to imprison us. He's trying to save us.

Scripture and prayer are two of the tools we have to learn from Jesus. Let this sink in: Christians actually believe that Jesus is alive and that He can speak with us through prayer and teach us how to live through the Scriptures. Jesus is real, active, and present. He is our rabbi, and He wants us to learn from Him. Yet many of us approach the Bible as a rule book or a history text that is outdated. Study can be seen as a chore or something to check off a to-do list. Prayer, too, is sometimes experienced as silent agony or as rehearsing a laundry list of problems. What if there were more to Scripture and prayer? I believe there is. As we come to live Jesus more deeply, we experience the joy that comes from moving in step with Him.

SERVICE

Mark 10:45 - "For even the Son of Man did not come to be served, but to serve, and to give his life as a ransom for many."

Service is simply putting someone else's needs above your own. It can be a large or a small gesture. It certainly doesn't have to be complicated. Look for a tangible way to serve someone today and then do it.

▼

1. What do you think Jesus meant by His invitation to "learn from me" in Matthew 11:29? How do we learn from Jesus?

2. What do you think Jesus meant in John 5:39-40? How should we approach the Scriptures? Is that how you are approaching them? Why/Why not?

3. What is the role of prayer in "learning from Jesus?"

4. Does it change the way we pray if we are trying to learn from Jesus? How so?

5. What is your prayer life like? What would it take for it to get better?

Read John 14:5-7, Matthew 11:27-30, and reflect on the week.
What has the Holy Spirit revealed to you this week?

SATURDAY | REST

"Our Souls are restless until they rest in God." *Augustine*

MAY - WEEK THREE

JESUS AS THE TRUTH

MONDAY - READ JOHN 14:5-7, JOHN 8:31-32, AND JOHN 18:38

At the end of John, Pilate stands in front of Jesus and asks a question for the ages: "What is truth?" This question is just as relevant today as it was in Pilate's time. We hear phrases like "that's my truth" or "you can believe your truth, and I'll believe mine." Truth—it seems—has come to signify nothing more than some set of beliefs or experiences that a person carries. Granted, this is a convenient way to understand truth; if it's just a set of beliefs that I determine for myself, then I'm responsible to no one but me, and I have complete authority over myself. The trouble is, humanity has proven time and time again that we don't make good masters. The first thing that happens when we are put in charge is that we mess things up.

Jesus offers a better way. Our Lord says, "I am the truth." And again He says, "The Son of Man is come to seek and to save that which was lost." Truth, therefore, is not hard to find for the very reason that it is seeking us![7]

So what is this truth that Jesus embodies? In the eighth chapter of John, Jesus tells us that knowing the truth will set us free. What is the truth we are to know in order to experience this freedom? Is it a list of facts or propositions? Jesus makes this statement in the midst of a larger conversation about doing what He says—obedience. If we do what we are commanded to do, He promises that we will know the truth and find true freedom. What if Jesus reveals more of Himself to people who were trying to live like Him? What if knowing Jesus depends on holding to His teaching? But, as A.W. Tozer points out, "it is not the difficulty of discovering truth but the unwillingness to obey it that makes it so rare among men."[8]

The point of knowing the truth isn't being able to rattle off a list of things about God. It's a fine thing to do, but it misses the point. If I were to make a life-sized cardboard cutout of my wife and write her personality traits on the back, that cut-out might display my knowledge about her—but it would definitely NOT be my wife. The only way to live in right relationship with my wife is to know the real thing. The same applies to God. His truth is so much more than a list of "do's" and "don'ts," "doctrines" and "theologies." It is a person: the person of Jesus. Sure, there are things about this person that we can and should know. But that's not the point. The point is knowing the truth like I know my wife.

We come to know the truth by living in the truth (living like Jesus) because when we live in Jesus, Jesus lives in us!

---

[7] *I got this idea from A.W. Tozer. It's considered public domain.*
[8] *This material is considered public domain.*

SERVICE

Mark 10:45 - "For even the Son of Man did not come to be served, but to serve, and to give his life as a ransom for many."

Service is simply putting someone else's needs above your own. It can be a large or a small gesture. It certainly doesn't have to be complicated. Look for a tangible way to serve someone today and then do it.

▼

1. How do you think the phrase "*You do you*" has impacted people's understanding of truth?
2. What changes in your understanding of truth when you hear that truth is looking for you?
3. If truth is a person, what does it mean that truth will set us free?
4. Do you agree that Jesus reveals more of Himself to those who are trying to live like Him? Why/Why not?

1. People think truths are personlize-able. They think that they are the deciders of what truth works for them.

2. It makes you see Full Truth and Love a person, not a set of ideas.

3. That only through God do we grasp truth. It's Him, Free from

4. the world's many ideas.

4. Yes, Jesus shows himself more to those who seek, ask, desire, search for Him. "Seek and ye shall find"

Read John 14:5-7, John 8:31-32, John 18:38 and reflect on the week.
What has the Holy Spirit revealed to you this week?

▼

oem?
?
Book!

John 14: 5-7 We can only get to the Father through Jesus, the truth, way life. Says to me... We need to take the "road of truth." That road is pure gold, true, solid, honest, reliable, holy.

John 8: 31-32 If you're holding onto Jesus, you're holding on to truth! You can't know the truth if you're not "holding to His teachings."

John 18:38 Pilate asked, "What is truth?" to the crowd. (as if they decide ... just like our world today ¨

This week, the Holy Spirit has impressed on me to let Him guide my way, ages, do list.

☆ There's a time to put aside my plans and trust His timing. (I wont to write!)

SATURDAY | REST

"We will never be at rest with less than God's
perfect abundance flowing into us each day."
Dr. Bud McCord "The Satisfying Life"

MAY - WEEK FOUR

JESUS AS THE LIFE

MONDAY - READ JOHN 14:5-7 AND JOHN 10:10

This week's portion of Scripture contains what is perhaps one of the best-known claims in the Bible: "I am the way, the truth, and the life." We've already discussed Jesus as the way and Jesus as the truth. But to get to Jesus as the life, I think it's important to make sure we don't miss the context of this rich passage. Within it, Jesus uses both wedding language and temple language. How can weddings and temples help us understand the life Jesus offers and how to live Jesus more abundantly?

First, let's explore the wedding language. After a Jewish man would ask a woman to marry him, he would go home to build an addition onto his family house. Multiple generations lived together in one large homestead. After this addition was finished, the man would return to get his bride and bring her to live with him. This is the imagery Jesus invokes by saying, "And if I go and prepare a place for you, I will come back and take you to be with me that you also may be where I am." By borrowing wedding language, Jesus is inviting the disciples to think about relationship, covenant, and intimacy.

But Jesus is also using temple language. "My Father's House" was a phrase used by Jesus to denote the temple (Luke 2:49, John 2:16). Throughout the Jewish story, the temple has served as a place where heaven and earth overlap. In Exodus, it was the traveling tent that denoted the presence of God. Later, it became a permanent place that was planned by David and constructed by Solomon. Within this temple was the "holy of holies"—a place where God Himself was said to live. In fact, if you asked any Jew where God's space was, they would point both to heaven and the temple. By using temple language, then, Jesus is inviting His disciples to think about God's unique presence with them in the world. He's God here, now, available.

Living in the presence of God (temple) and in right relationship with God (wedding) is what humanity is designed to do. It describes life and it to the full. John opens his Gospel by telling us that the Word became flesh and "templed" among us. Jesus IS the place where we live in right relationship with God while enjoying His presence. Jesus gives us life and shows us how to live it!

SERVICE

▼

Mark 10:45 - "For even the Son of Man did not come to be served, but to serve, and to give his life as a ransom for many."

Service is simply putting someone else's needs above your own. It can be a large or a small gesture. It certainly doesn't have to be complicated. Look for a tangible way to serve someone today and then do it.

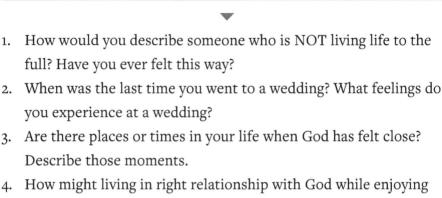

1. How would you describe someone who is NOT living life to the full? Have you ever felt this way?
2. When was the last time you went to a wedding? What feelings do you experience at a wedding?
3. Are there places or times in your life when God has felt close? Describe those moments.
4. How might living in right relationship with God while enjoying God's presence describe life to the full?
5. How do we gain this kind of life? Does everyone have access to it? What prevents us from enjoying it?

Read John 14:5-7, John 10:10, and reflect on the week.
What has the Holy Spirit revealed to you this week?

SATURDAY | REST

*"If we stop, if we return to rest, our natural
state reasserts itself. Our natural wisdom and
balance come to our aid, and we can find our
way to what is good, necessary and true."*
Wayne Muller "Sacred Rhythms"

JUNE - WEEK ONE

JESUS AS THE POWER TO WITNESS

MONDAY - READ ACTS 1:8 AND ACTS 19:1-6

A few years ago, a large tree next to my house split in two, and the top half landed on my porch. I felt the whole house shake and went outside to see what had happened. My first response was "Wow we're so lucky that didn't land on our house!" My next thought was "What a mess to clean up!" I got out my hand saw and cut a few branches. The work was back-breaking, so I called a friend who came over with a chainsaw. The difference was so stark: I didn't want to use a hand saw ever again! In this day and age, hardly anyone would do a major construction job without power tools. However, many of us are still trying to live a spiritual life with only the equivalent of a hand saw. We're trying to do it all by ourselves, outside of the power the Spirit gives. This month, we'll be focusing in on the power that Jesus offers. This week, we'll discuss one particular facet of that: the power we have to tell others about our experience with Jesus.

Just before Jesus was to ascend to the Father, His disciples gathered around Him and received this promise: "You will receive power when the Holy Spirit comes on you." The word translated as power is the Greek word dynamis, from which we get the word "dynamite." This promise is made in the context of Jesus asking for witnesses: people testifying about their experience with Him. Sometimes witnessing can be difficult. We don't know what to say. There are closed doors that we cannot open. Then there's the fact that our lives often don't live up to our testimony. Perhaps we think that people will consider us to be hypocritical, arrogant, dimwitted, or fanatical. All of these factors add up to what seems like an immovable mountain, an obstacle too big to overcome. But let's hear the words of Jesus anew: "You will receive DYNAMITE when the Holy Spirit comes on you."

When we deny this dynamic power, not only are we making the Christian life harder than it has to be, but we are also not being faithful witnesses to Jesus— or even truly living the Christian life at all! Perhaps this is why Paul insists on baptizing some disciples again when he hears that they did not receive the Holy Spirit. These men said they had only received the baptism of John, which is a baptism of repentance.

I think there are many Christians who have only received the baptism of repentance. They have confessed their sins and asked Jesus to save them. But repentance is only the beginning of the story. There is a power that is waiting to be unleashed in you. Ask the Spirit today for the power to testify to His goodness in your life.

CONFESSION

James 5:16 - "Therefore confess your sins to each other and pray for each other so that you may be healed. The prayer of a righteous person is powerful and effective."

Confession can be scary. But here, James pairs it with prayer as a pathway to healing. Sin is like a disease that keeps you from living life to the full. It is something that grieves the Holy Spirit and prevents God from doing what He wants to do in you and through you. Sunlight is said to be one of the best disinfectants. Confession is like letting the light into a deep sin-infection. It cleans and it heals. Today, choose a trusted friend and confess a sin to them. Maybe you want to start small. But don't be afraid to be honest. I'll bet you'll find that you're not alone.

▼

1. What does it feel like to try to live the Christian life without the power of the Holy Spirit?
2. Why do you think we attempt to "go it alone" without the help of the Holy Spirit?
3. How do we access this help of the Holy Spirit? What role do we play in other people's lives in helping them receive the Holy Spirit (i.e. what role did Paul play in Acts 19:1-6)?
4. What does it mean to be a witness?
5. What are some reasons people do not witness? How does the Holy Spirit help us overcome these obstacles?

....

....

....

....

....

....

....

....

....

....

....

Read Acts 1:8, Acts 19:1-6, and reflect on the week.
What has the Holy Spirit revealed to you this week?

SATURDAY | REST

"Remain in me, as I also remain in you." John 15:4

JUNE - WEEK TWO

JESUS AS THE POWER TO BELONG

MONDAY - READ 1 CORINTHIANS 12

The Holy Spirit is the best gift we could receive, because it allows Jesus's very power to work in us. We can't lose sight of this big gift as we turn toward another related topic today: the gifts of the Spirit. Each one of us has been given the power to witness by the Holy Spirit, and one way we do this is through using the unique gifts He gives us to accomplish His mission.

When God wanted to reach into the world with His heart of mission and redemption, He became human. In other words, He put on a particular body in order to reach everybody. God still uses a body to reach into the world and it's still the body of Jesus. This is exactly the metaphor Paul uses in 1 Corinthians 12 when talking about the Church: "Now you are the body of Christ and each one of you is a part of it." The "you" Paul is speaking about is not you, individually; he's saying, "y'all are the body of Christ."

Spiritual gifts give you the power to belong to the body of Christ in a unique way: a way that only you can belong. As you find your place in the body and exercise your gifts, you help the body of Jesus accomplish its mission on earth! We might not all do street evangelism, but some will, and others hospitably receive those who come into the church. Some will speak on a public-facing platform, while others will provide the infrastructure ("helps") that enables them to do so effectively. As we use the gifts we have been given, we testify to the goodness of God to us and to our desire to live Jesus more abundantly. Indeed, we become witnesses to the life of Jesus when we take part in the life of His body, the Church.

God is making us into His body by giving us the gift of His Spirit. Then, just as He sent Jesus out, He sends the Church body to bring about His redemptive purposes. Therefore, the spiritual gifts we are given are not for us. They are to be used for God's mission in the world through the body of Christ. You have a role to play in this. Y'all includes you!

CONFESSION

James 5:16 - "Therefore confess your sins to each other and pray for each other so that you may be healed. The prayer of a righteous person is powerful and effective."

Confession can be scary. But here, James pairs it with prayer as a pathway to healing. Sin is like a disease that keeps you from living life to the full. It is something that grieves the Holy Spirit and prevents God from doing what He wants to do in you and through you. Sunlight is said to be one of the best disinfectants. Confession is like letting the light into a deep sin-infection. It cleans and it heals. Today, choose a trusted friend and confess a sin to them. Maybe you want to start small. But don't be afraid to be honest. I'll bet you'll find that you're not alone.

▼

1. Do you believe you play a valuable role in the body of Christ? Why/Why not? What would you say your role is? Are you stepping up to that role?

2. Often, spiritual gifts are spoken of as though they are special abilities that people have. What changes if you instead view spiritual gifts as pieces that are meant to fit together to accomplish God's mission through God's body?

3. Why do you think the Holy Spirit doesn't just give everyone all of the gifts?

4. Another way to ask question 2: What is your spiritual gift? How are you using it to help the church fulfill God's mission in the world?

5. Helpful exercise: Find someone you trust and help each other discover your spiritual gifts (through a test or through conversation).

Read 1 Corinthians 12 and reflect on the week.
What has the Holy Spirit revealed to you this week?

▼

SATURDAY | REST

"Now remain in my love." John 15:9b

JUNE - WEEK THREE

JESUS AS THE POWER TO LIVE A HOLY LIFE

MONDAY - READ GALATIANS 5:16-25

Living Jesus, we have seen, is a communal affair—we do it together, in the company of other believers whose gifts complement one another. At the same time, as we in our many parts together grow in grace, so also does Jesus grow each of us to fullness, so that we become wholly and completely the individual person He created us to be.

In this famous passage, Paul describes the fruit of the Spirit. These are the qualities that people who are walking in accordance with the Holy Spirit display. People who live Jesus bear abundant fruit with all these characteristics: love, joy, peace, and so on. An apple is not an apple unless it has all its characteristics—color, taste, texture, skin, flesh, and seeds—and so also is the fruit of the Spirit a whole package, one fruit with an abundance of descriptors that those who walk with God make evident.

> **"**
> **When the Holy Spirit is alive and active in your life, you will demonstrate the whole fruit of the Spirit.** **"**

Sometimes, though, it seems that people interpret each of these characteristics to be a separate fruit. It is as though I might ask the Spirit for a little joy or self-control because I'm running low today — but skip the patience because I just don't feel like waiting! While I don't think there is anything wrong with asking the Spirit for more joy or self-control, I also don't think that is a helpful way to approach the fruit of the Spirit.

These qualities are together the evidence of the work of the Holy Spirit in your life. Fruit of the Spirit is singular, not plural: it is all present or all lacking. When the Holy Spirit is alive and active in your life, you will demonstrate the whole fruit of the Spirit. This is why Paul doesn't simply instruct us to ask for various fruits in increasing measure. No, he tells us to crucify the flesh and walk with the Spirit. It's not, "I'll take a little peace today, please." Instead it's, "I crucify my flesh today—all of its desires, tastes, and longings and I ask instead to be filled with the life of the Spirit."

As we abandon our daily lives, we are added to the Spirit. We put our whole selves into the hands of God and there is a murder or death that happens; we lose our old selves in order to be filled with the Spirit. The evidence of this is the fruit of the Spirit: love, joy, peace, patience, kindness, goodness, gentleness, faithfulness, and self-control. If any of this is lacking, it is because we have yet to crucify our flesh with its passions and desires.

When we live this kind of life, we become witnesses for Jesus because we start to live the kind of life Jesus would live if He were in our shoes. The people around us notice our love, joy, peace, patience, kindness, goodness, faithfulness, gentleness, and self-control. In other words, we live a holy life.

Holy simply means "set apart." The point of being set apart isn't to keep the world at arm's length. Jesus did not keep the world away. Rather, He was lifted up so the world could see what it was made for. His holiness was a part of His mission. And it's also a part of ours.

CONFESSION

James 5:16 - "Therefore confess your sins to each other and pray for each other so that you may be healed. The prayer of a righteous person is powerful and effective."

Confession can be scary. But here, James pairs it with prayer as a pathway to healing. Sin is like a disease that keeps you from living life to the full. It is something that grieves the Holy Spirit and prevents God from doing what He wants to do in you and through you. Sunlight is said to be one of the best disinfectants. Confession is like letting the light into a deep sin-infection. It cleans and it heals. Today, choose a trusted friend and confess a sin to them. Maybe you want to start small. But don't be afraid to be honest. I'll bet you'll find that you're not alone.

1. What is your initial understanding of holiness? What did it mean to you growing up in church (or not growing up in church)?

2. Do you believe that the way we live impacts our ability to witness? Why/Why not?

3. Can the fruit of the Spirit sum up the way Jesus lived? Is it possible to live like Jesus? How?

4. What changes for you if the fruit of the Spirit is seen as a whole rather than segmented gifts of the Spirit? What does it mean for the whole fruit if one (or multiple) aspects of that fruit is missing from your life?

5. How is a person filled with the Spirit? How does this filling help a person bear the fruit of the Spirit?

Read Galatians 5:16-25 and reflect on the week.
What has the Holy Spirit revealed to you this week?

▼

SATURDAY | REST

"My Presence will go with you, and I will give you rest."
Exodus 33:14

JUNE - WEEK FOUR

JESUS AS THE POWER TO SEE

MONDAY - READ JOHN 16:7-15 AND ACTS 10:36-44

In our first passage, we see the sadness of the disciples at the news of Jesus's departure. But for Jesus, this is not something to grieve over. Rather, He sees it as an opportunity to send the Holy Spirit. The Holy Spirit's job is to 1) help the disciples remember Jesus's teaching and 2) glorify Jesus in the world. The Holy Spirit is all about Jesus! Perhaps this is why the Spirit comes in such a powerful way when Peter is speaking about Him in Acts.

In this second passage, we see a perfect set-up for a powerful testimony to the work of Jesus in Peter's life. There is a Gentile who wants to know about Jesus. Peter is summoned, and he preaches to them. He starts with telling them about Jesus—who He was, what He was doing, and how He fit in God's long salvation story. Then, we are told that WHILE HE WAS STILL SPEAKING, the Holy Spirit falls upon the people listening.

Now, I am not saying that we can control the Spirit. Jesus tells us that the Holy Spirit is like the wind—you can't control where and when it blows. However, there seem to be conditions that increase the likelihood of the Holy Spirit's coming. Throughout Acts, the Spirit is poured out whenever people are speaking about Jesus as Lord. It's almost like the Holy Spirit says, "yes and amen!" every time Jesus is lifted up.

You are going through a year of declaring your desire to see, live, hear, and love Jesus. This is a desire the Holy Spirit aids. When you declare your desire to see Jesus, the Spirit reveals Christ around you, in you, and through you. When you pray to hear the words of Jesus, the Holy Spirit is there to remind you of everything He said. When you ask for the power to live like Jesus in front of a watching world (or family or co-workers or anyone else in your circle of influence), the Holy Spirit is right there to empower you to do it. When you long for Jesus and your heart aches to love Him more, the Holy Spirit draws close and enables you to experience the presence of Jesus. These are the things the Holy Spirit does. Thank you, Jesus, for the gift of the Spirit!

CONFESSION

James 5:16 - "Therefore confess your sins to each other and pray for each other so that you may be healed. The prayer of a righteous person is powerful and effective."

Confession can be scary. But here, James pairs it with prayer as a pathway to healing. Sin is like a disease that keeps you from living life to the full. It is something that grieves the Holy Spirit and prevents God from doing what He wants to do in you and through you. Sunlight is said to be one of the best disinfectants. Confession is like letting the light into a deep sin-infection. It cleans and it heals. Today, choose a trusted friend and confess a sin to them. Maybe you want to start small. But don't be afraid to be honest. I'll bet you'll find that you're not alone.

▼

. What is your experience with the Holy Spirit?

2. If you are lacking Holy Spirit encounters, why should you start by lifting up Jesus? What does it mean to lift up Jesus?

3. Have you ever experienced an outpouring of the Holy Spirit while you were witnessing (in word or in deed)? What did it feel like? Can you describe the moment? What was the reaction of the people involved?

4. Why do you think the people in Cornelius's household asked Peter to stay with them a few more days after the Holy Spirit fell on them (Acts 10:48)? Didn't they have everything they needed in the Holy Spirit? Why did they need Peter?

5. Why were Peter's companions astonished that the Holy Spirit fell on the Gentiles (Acts 10:45)? Are there people in your life that you have deemed "unworthy" of the gift of the Holy Spirit? Why do we have a tendency to do this? How do we overcome this mindset?

Read John 16:7-15, Acts 10:36-44, and reflect on the week.
What has the Holy Spirit revealed to you this week?

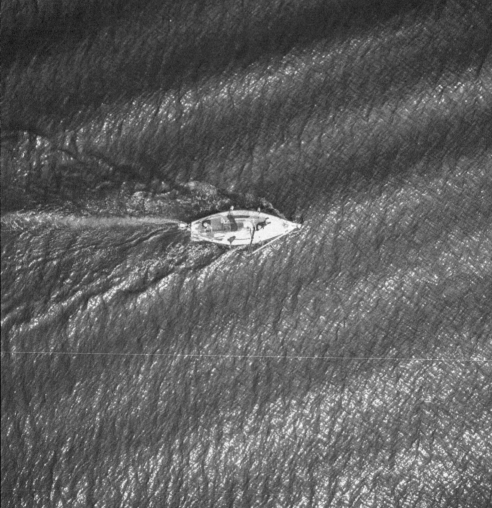

JULY - WEEK ONE

JESUS AS CAPTAIN

MONDAY - READ LUKE 5:1-3 FOCUS ON VS. 3

During the next three months, we are going to focus on hearing Jesus more. Just as seeing Him and living Him can happen in unexpected ways, so also can we sometimes hear His voice coming from places we don't anticipate. In today's passage, Simon first hears it in a simple request from a man who wanted to borrow a tool.

I'm pretty sure the only thing I can fix is a sandwich. I get all frustrated and nervous any time I am required to do even the most menial of home repairs. One winter, my wife and I decided to use our tax refund to remodel our bathroom. I did all the research I knew how to do (which was simply looking it up on Youtube). We tore up the floor, cut new baseboards, installed the toilet and vanity. After all of this work, the sink leaked! I tried my best, but no matter what I did, I couldn't get the sink to stop leaking.

Finally, I broke down and had to phone a friend. He is a plumber that goes to church with me. He came over and spent about five seconds under my sink, and it no longer leaked! I was shocked and a little embarrassed. To be honest, I wanted him to sweat and grunt as he attempted to accomplish the most difficult plumbing job he had ever encountered. Nope, it was easy. I was using the same tools that he used. But they accomplished more in his hands than in mine.

Simon has a tool of the trade he used: a fishing boat. But on the day Jesus asks to use Simon's boat, that boat becomes more useful than it has ever been before—it becomes a podium. It isn't that the boat stops being a boat or gains any extra boat qualities. Jesus just uses its "boat-ness" in a way that expands its usefulness, just as my plumbing tools expanded their usefulness in the hands of my plumber-friend. He could use them in ways that I simply couldn't.

So let me ask you a question: "Can Jesus use your boat?" Before you say that you don't have a boat and you prefer to have friends who have boats, let me unpack that question. With his boat, Simon earns money, makes relationships, and establishes an identity. The very fact that he is fishing probably means that his father fished and his grandfather before him fished as well. The boat, then, represents financial well-being, a relational network, family history, vocational identity, sweat, tears, and joy. The boat would have been at the center of Simon's whole life. Now, hear the question Jesus asked Simon again: "Can I use your boat?" Does Jesus have access to every resource of your life? Have you invited Him into the center of your existence as your captain?

SOLITUDE

▼

Matthew 14:22-23 - "Immediately Jesus made the disciples get into the boat and go on ahead of him to the other side, while he dismissed the crowd. After he had dismissed them, he went up on a mountainside by himself to pray. Later that night, he was there alone,"

Jesus sent people away; He created space to be alone. Today, we are asking you to plan to be alone for a whole hour. It might mean turning off your cell phone and going for a walk. It may mean staying up for an hour after your family is in bed. There is a chance you will have to plan this in advance and communicate your plan to your family. But if Jesus thought solitude was important, maybe we should too.

The Scripture for this month focuses on the call of Jesus. You should use this time of solitude to listen for Jesus's call. Is He inviting you to follow Him anywhere? Is He inviting you closer to Him?

▼

1. What do you think Simon/Peter was thinking when Jesus just got into his boat? What would you think if someone just got into your car and told you to drive somewhere?

2. Jesus could have walked on water. Why do you think Jesus chose to use Simon's boat instead of walking on water?

3. Simon's boat was his life—it was his source of income and the place he spent most of his day/night. What is your "boat"?

4. Do you believe Jesus wants to get into your "boat" or just watch you live your life from a distance? Why?

5. Have you invited Jesus into your "boat?" How do we do that?

Read Luke 5:1-3 and reflect on the week.
What has the Holy Spirit revealed to you this week?

SATURDAY | REST

*"Whoever dwells in the shelter of the Most
High will rest in the shadow of the Almighty. I
will say of the Lord, 'He is my refuge and my
fortress, my God, in whom I trust.'"*
Psalm 91:1-2

JULY - WEEK TWO

JESUS AS GUIDE

MONDAY - READ LUKE 5:1-5 AND EPHESIANS 2:1-10

"Put out into deep water." That just sounds scary. We are used to shallow water. I can play in shallow water. I can splash and feel the comfort of the water without any of the danger. After all, if something happens, I am able to put my feet down—I can touch the ground. Deep water is dangerous. Deep water holds mystery. Jesus calls Simon Peter into this mystery.

This call comes by way of a command that doesn't make sense—"Put out into deep water and let down the nets for a catch." First, these fishermen fish at night in shallow water. They do this so they can see the fish reflecting the light from the moon. Fishing in the afternoon would be like fishing blind. Second, Simon Peter was most likely using shallow water fishing nets that were meant to catch shallow water fish. To make matters worse, Simon Peter had fished all night and had already cleaned his nets. He was exhausted and ready to go home. Yet Simon Peter pushes out into deep water because Jesus says so. There's the key: "because Jesus says so." The word of Jesus is a doorway for Peter's faith.

Usually when we hear the word "faith," we think along the lines of belief. But faith doesn't mean belief. It means trust. In a trust fall, it's the difference between believing in your head that the person behind you will catch you and actually taking the risk of falling backwards into the person's arms. When we are saved by grace through faith, it is not that we believe our way to God's free gift of salvation. Instead, it means that we are saved by the power of God when we risk everything and trust in that power—and only that power—to save us. Grace is the means and faith is the way. Let's go back to the trust fall exercise. I have to believe that there is a person behind me who can catch me. However, my belief doesn't turn into faith until I fall backwards into that person's arms. Then I am trusting in the unseen power of the person behind me to hold me up.

Simon puts his faith in Jesus. This leads to doing what Jesus says to do because faith (trust) and obedience are two sides of the same coin. Perhaps after hearing Jesus teach that morning, Simon has come to trust that Jesus knows more about how to operate in the world than he does. So when Jesus (a carpenter) tells Simon (a fisherman) how to fish, Simon obeys even though it seems crazy. Simon hears and does accordingly. How do you hear Jesus calling to you?

SOLITUDE

▼

Matthew 14:22-23 - "Immediately Jesus made the disciples get into the boat and go on ahead of him to the other side, while he dismissed the crowd. After he had dismissed them, he went up on a mountainside by himself to pray. Later that night, he was there alone,"

Jesus sent people away; He created space to be alone. Today, we are asking you to plan to be alone for a whole hour. It might mean turning off your cell phone and going for a walk. It may mean staying up for an hour after your family is in bed. There is a chance you will have to plan this in advance and communicate your plan to your family. But if Jesus thought solitude was important, maybe we should too.

The Scripture for this month focuses on the call of Jesus. You should use this time of solitude to listen for Jesus's call. Is He inviting you to follow Him anywhere? Is He inviting you closer to Him?

▼

1. In your own words, what does it mean to have faith in Jesus?
2. In general, why is obedience difficult (to parents, bosses, etc)? Why is it difficult to obey Jesus?
3. How is deeper surrender related to deeper faith?
4. Where do you feel Jesus inviting you to practice deeper faith?

Read Luke 5:1-5, Ephesians 2:1-10, and reflect on the week.
What has the Holy Spirit revealed to you this week?

SATURDAY | REST

"Sabbath is that uncluttered time and space in which we can distance ourselves from our own activities enough to see what God is doing."
Eugene Peterson, *The Pastor's Guide to Personal Spiritual Formation*

JESUS AS THE FISHER OF MEN

MONDAY - READ LUKE 5:1-6 AND MATTHEW 4:18-22

There is a miracle in this story! Peter obeys Jesus and then catches so many fish that the nets are about to burst and the boats almost sink. It is this miracle that prompts Peter to say, "Go away from me, I am a sinful man." Jesus does the opposite though. He comes closer, inviting Peter deeper into discipleship. That's no surprise, really—Jesus always responds to our obedience by revealing more of Himself by inviting us to come near. So Jesus's call to Peter is an invitation to work alongside Him, not just to know a few things or perform a few tasks.

In Peter's case, the call is to evangelism specifically—and evangelism is part of our invitation as well. When Jesus calls Peter, He asks him to become a fisher of men. The miraculous catch on the fishing boat becomes a sign for the kind of life into which Jesus is inviting Peter. Fishing in Jesus's time was done with nets, and when Jesus calls Peter to be a "fisher of men," this is the image He has in mind.

If evangelism is like net-fishing, then it's NOT baiting a hook, casting a line, and reeling someone in. Yet all too often we seem to think we have to find just the right "bait" to get people to swallow our "hook"; sometimes this means we try hard to make the Gospel "palatable" or "seeker-friendly" or inoffensive. We focus on safe topics like love and acceptance and avoid difficult questions; we make sure all our programs are both fun and relevant, and we load our websites with slick graphics. It's not bad to think about how what we're doing will be received by those we hope to reach—but we're also not responsible for reeling people in with just the right bait. We most definitely do not need to rewrite the Gospel to make it more appealing. Jesus wants us simply to "let down our nets for a catch."

This kind of evangelism means the Church goes where the people are, wraps its arms around them, and brings them into the fold. Those who were outside are now considered inside. As people are wrapped into the life of the church, they experience the love of Christ and the transformation of the Gospel. This is our task—to go fishing for people. Yes, we have pressed out into deep waters. But while we are in deep waters, we hear the voice of Jesus asking us to let down the nets for a catch!

SOLITUDE

▼

Matthew 14:22-23 - "Immediately Jesus made the disciples get into the boat and go on ahead of him to the other side, while he dismissed the crowd. After he had dismissed them, he went up on a mountainside by himself to pray. Later that night, he was there alone,"

Jesus sent people away; He created space to be alone. Today, we are asking you to plan to be alone for a whole hour. It might mean turning off your cell phone and going for a walk. It may mean staying up for an hour after your family is in bed. There is a chance you will have to plan this in advance and communicate your plan to your family. But if Jesus thought solitude was important, maybe we should too.

The Scripture for this month focuses on the call of Jesus. You should use this time of solitude to listen for Jesus's call. Is He inviting you to follow Him anywhere? Is He inviting you closer to Him?

1. What did Jesus mean when He told Peter He would make him a fisher of men?
2. There are a few ways to fish (or do evangelism). Do you believe people are sick of hook-line-and-sinker kind of evangelism? What characterizes this kind of evangelism?
3. How is it different to see evangelism along the lines of fishing with a net than fishing with a hook?
4. How can you wrap your arms around those with needs and bring them into the "boat?"

Read Luke 5:1-6, Matthew 4:18-22, and reflect on the week.
What has the Holy Spirit revealed to you this week?

▼

SATURDAY | REST

"Are you tired? Worn out? Burned out on religion? Come to me. Get away with me and you'll recover your life. I'll show you how to take a real rest. Walk with me and work with me— watch how I do it. Learn the unforced rhythms of grace. I won't lay anything heavy or ill-fitting on you. Keep company with me and you'll learn to live freely and lightly."
Matthew 11:28-30 (The Message)

JULY - WEEK FOUR

JESUS AS THE LEGACY

MONDAY - READ LUKE 5:1-11 AND PSALM 145:1-7

What happens to that miraculous catch? Go ahead, read it (Luke 5:11). Two boatloads of fish would not only have provided food for Simon Peter's family but a huge paycheck as well. But instead of taking all that for himself, Simon appears to leave God's provision on the shore for other people to enjoy. How is Simon able to leave his largest catch for other people? It's because Jesus gives him a vocation in the kingdom of heaven. Simon is invited to join God in kingdom expansion. That call is louder than any voice from his past urging him to stay in his boat.

We all want to be a part of something bigger than we are currently. I think we can sometimes think of Simon as super-spiritual. He forsakes that large pile of fish for a life of wandering as a homeless man with Jesus. But we have to remember that Peter thinks that a life with Jesus is BETTER than a life lived on his own. He is convinced that Jesus is offering him something much better than a huge paycheck. Simon Peter believes that a life with Jesus will be a bigger, more significant life than what he has with his family on the familiar shores of Galilee. This should not be lost on us.

When we speak of living a life that is bigger than us, we are speaking about legacy. Peter could have sold those fish and enjoyed life for a while. Maybe he would have been famous as the "person who brought in the largest catch ever." Maybe other fishermen would have whispered his name in awe as he walked past them. But Simon Peter heard Jesus's call to a life that was larger than that. If we're going to leave a lasting legacy, we too have to hear Him invite us into something that is bigger than us. We have to catch a vision of a life lived with Jesus!

SOLITUDE

▼

Matthew 14:22-23 - "Immediately Jesus made the disciples get into the boat and go on ahead of him to the other side, while he dismissed the crowd. After he had dismissed them, he went up on a mountainside by himself to pray. Later that night, he was there alone,"

Jesus sent people away; He created space to be alone. Today, we are asking you to plan to be alone for a whole hour. It might mean turning off your cell phone and going for a walk. It may mean staying up for an hour after your family is in bed. There is a chance you will have to plan this in advance and communicate your plan to your family. But if Jesus thought solitude was important, maybe we should too.

The Scripture for this month focuses on the call of Jesus. You should use this time of solitude to listen for Jesus's call. Is He inviting you to follow Him anywhere? Is He inviting you closer to Him?

▼

1. What might happen if we focused less on earning and more on loving God and others?

2. What do you think John Wesley meant by this quote: "...do not send your children to hell by leaving them your wealth. Have pity on them"?

3. What kind of legacy is Wesley talking about leaving your children?

4. In what ways does leaving a legacy of faith impact those who come behind you?

5. What would be your legacy if you were to pass away today? Can that change? How?

Read Luke 5:1-11, Psalm 145:1-7, and reflect on the week.
What has the Holy Spirit revealed to you this week?

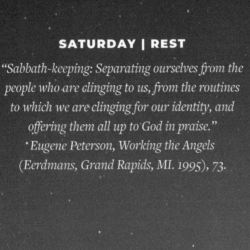

SATURDAY | REST

"Sabbath-keeping: Separating ourselves from the people who are clinging to us, from the routines to which we are clinging for our identity, and offering them all up to God in praise."
Eugene Peterson, Working the Angels (Eerdmans, Grand Rapids, MI. 1995), 73.

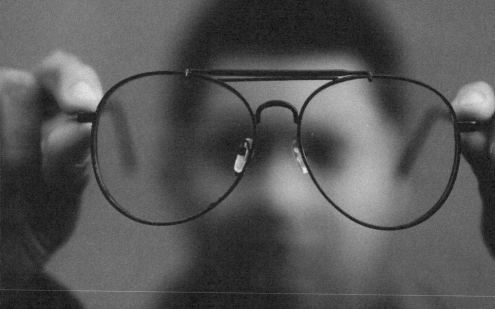

AUGUST - WEEK ONE

JESUS as OUR VISION

MONDAY - READ MATTHEW 9:35-38 AND MATTHEW 20:29-34

Do we see people? It is entirely possible to go from our living rooms where we watch T.V., to our vehicles where we listen to music, to our workplace where we bury our noses in our phones, computer screens, or to-do-lists...and completely ignore the people around us. Perhaps the first movement toward compassion—the focus of this month's discussions—includes learning to see like Jesus sees.

In this week's passage, we are told that Jesus moves from village to village. How do you think Jesus gets around? He walks. Jesus moves slowly enough to notice the needs around Him. This is illustrated in Matthew 20. Jesus is about to pass by, and two blind men are suddenly interested—what if He can heal them? They start making a lot of noise, and what does the crowd do? It tells them to be quiet. But Jesus hears, stops, and calls them closer. These men are invisible to society except as people getting in the way and causing a distraction. But Jesus sees them.

By contrast, we prefer to move quickly from place to place in order to check off tasks on our to-do lists. We are usually too interested in where we are going to stop and notice the people on the way. We might even "shoosh" them! I'm afraid that we don't move slowly enough to be moved by compassion.

Eugene Peterson was a pastor, author, and professor at Regent College. He was already famous when he was teaching at Regent because of the many books he had written. Surely he was a big name on campus. However, he routinely left for every class 20 minutes early so that he could stop and talk to students on his way. He learned every student's name in the divinity school of over 200 students. He also knew the names of their spouses and children. He was famous! He didn't have to do this. But he walked slowly and purposefully so that he could pay attention to people.

How deliberately do we pay attention to other people? When you fill up at the gas station, do you see who is at the pump beside you? When you walk into a store through the parking lot, do you notice those walking the other direction? How well do you know the person you work next to at the office? When you take a walk with your kids, how do you help them learn to see better? The call to compassion is first a call to slow down and see people. May we commit together that there will be no invisible people in our lives.

SIMPLICITY

▼

Matthew 6:21-34 - "So do not worry, saying, 'What shall we eat?' or 'What shall we drink?' or 'What shall we wear?' For the pagans run after all these things, and your heavenly Father knows that you need them. But seek first his kingdom and his righteousness, and all these things will be given to you as well. Therefore do not worry about tomorrow, for tomorrow will worry about itself. Each day has enough trouble of its own."

Simplicity is about seeking first the Kingdom of Heaven. We don't have to add things to our lives because we have Jesus! Here's your challenge for today: Don't buy something. It could be a candy bar or a sofa. Either way, the challenge is to seek first the Kingdom and remember that you don't need extra stuff.

1. Why do you think everyone appears so "busy"? Is it comfortable to NOT be busy? Why/why not?

2. What does compassion mean? Can you think of a time when you saw it/experienced it?

3. Why does compassion require us to see people? How does slowing down help us see other people?

4. Even when we see other people, it is sometimes difficult to see their need. Why is this?

5. How can you become more attentive to other people's needs?

....

....

....

....

....

....

....

....

....

....

....

Read Matthew 9:35-38, Matthew 20:29-34, and reflect on the week.
What has the Holy Spirit revealed to you this week?

▼

SATURDAY | REST

*"Sabbath-keeping: Quieting the internal
noise so we hear the still small voice of our
Lord. Removing the distractions of pride so we
discern the presence of Christ."*
Eugene Peterson, *Working the Angels*
(Eerdmans, Grand Rapids, MI. 1995), 73

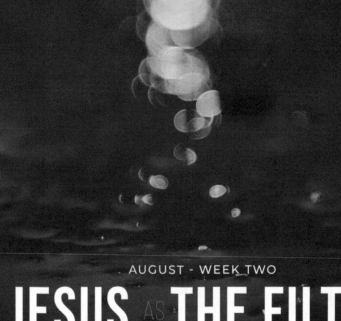

AUGUST - WEEK TWO

JESUS AS THE FILTER

MONDAY - READ MATTHEW 9:35-38 AND MARK 1:40-44

When Jesus slows down to see people, what does He see? I think His filter is different from ours. This is demonstrated when He encounters a leper who asks if Jesus is willing to heal him. Jesus responds to that question in a way that probably surprises us. He gets angry.

At face value, there are a couple reasons that Jesus might be angry. First, He might be angry because this man is bothering Him. Jesus is on His way somewhere and He has just healed a lot of people. Perhaps He is tired and doesn't want to heal one more. But Jesus has been "bothered" like this many times in the Gospel stories and we never see that He gets angry about it. So I don't think that is the reason. Second, He might be angry that the man has leprosy and is so close to Him. This man disobeys cleanliness laws and risks exposing Jesus to a deadly disease. But Jesus immediately reaches out and touches him—so that doesn't seem to be a problem either.

I think the reason Jesus is angry has to do with the ways this man has suffered. Because people do not see him as a child of God, but as "unclean" and "unworthy," this man has lived in a world where he has had to question his worth and value. No wonder Jesus is angry. Jesus, the creator, made this man—and Jesus loves him.

If any one of my children approached me after being ravaged by the world, wearing filthy rags and showing signs of abuse, I would be angry too—how has this happened to them? I would get closer to them and ask why they didn't come to me sooner. If they told me that they didn't think I would care or that they hadn't been sure I would help them, I would ask, "WHO TOLD YOU THAT?" I would wonder who lied to them. I would be angry both at how they'd been treated and that they believed themselves to be unworthy of my attention. I think this kind of value-filter is what made Jesus so angry. I think it still makes Him angry.

When Jesus sees the crowd, He doesn't see nuisances or an opportunity to demonstrate His power and prove His worth. He sees people who are harassed and helpless. Sometimes there are people in our lives we have trouble looking on with eyes of compassion. But what if we saw them as Jesus sees them? If they are harassed, they have an enemy—and that means they're not the enemy! If they're helpless, it means there's nothing more they can do. In other words, they are doing the best they can. This is the filter through which Jesus sees. It's the filter He invites us to put on.

SIMPLICITY

▼

Matthew 6:21-34 - "So do not worry, saying, 'What shall we eat?' or 'What shall we drink?' or 'What shall we wear?' For the pagans run after all these things, and your heavenly Father knows that you need them. But seek first his kingdom and his righteousness, and all these things will be given to you as well. Therefore do not worry about tomorrow, for tomorrow will worry about itself. Each day has enough trouble of its own."

Simplicity is about seeking first the Kingdom of Heaven. We don't have to add things to our lives because we have Jesus! Here's your challenge for today: Don't buy something. It could be a candy bar or a sofa. Either way, the challenge is to seek first the Kingdom and remember that you don't need extra stuff.

▼

1. What does it mean to get your value from what other people think of you?

2. Describe what it feels like to live in a world where you are unsure of your value.

3. How does seeing people as valuable help us see them with eyes of compassion?

4. How does having your own value settled with God enable you to respond with compassion?

5. What does Jesus see when He looks at you?

Read Matthew 9:35-38, Mark 1:40-44, and reflect on the week.
What has the Holy Spirit revealed to you this week?

SATURDAY | REST

*"Rest is not a hallowed feeling that comes over us in
church; it is the repose of a heart set deep in God."*
Drummond

AUGUST - WEEK THREE

JESUS AS COMPASSION

MONDAY - READ MATTHEW 9:35-38 AND MATTHEW 14:13-16

Once we have learned to see with compassion, we cannot help but hear the invitation Jesus gives us to reach out. The Greek word that is translated to compassion is "splagchnizomai" (pronounced splänkh-ne'-zo-mi). It means to be moved as in one's bowels. For the ancients, the guts were where the most intense and intimate emotions were located, the center from which both love and hate grew. Today we talk about the heart as the center of our feelings; they talked about their guts. So when the Gospels speak of Jesus's compassion, they are saying He was moved deep in His guts, in the most vulnerable part of His being.

This Greek word is related quite closely with the Hebrew word for compassion, "rachamim." But instead of the "guts," the Hebrew word refers to the "womb" of Yahweh. Compassion is such a deep and powerful emotion in Jesus that it can only be described as a movement in the womb of God—the place of utmost growth, creativity, and love. When something hits in a deep place like the womb of God, you know that something is about to happen. Wombs bring forth new life.

In our portion of Scripture, Jesus is having a terrible day. His cousin has just been beheaded, so He goes away to a private place to mourn. But the crowds follow Him, and they stay. And they stay longer. And they stay longer—until they are badly in need of some dinner. Throughout this episode, Jesus is able to see the crowds through a lens of compassion, and even as the disciples are pressing Him to send the crowds away, He responds by inviting them closer. Compassion also leads Jesus to do something about their physical needs. This "something" ends up being one of the greatest miracles recorded: the feeding of the 5000.

Compassion invites us not to isolate or insulate ourselves but to reach out. It asks us to go where it hurts and to enter into the brokenness, fear, and confusion of other people. After all, this is how Jesus responds to us. He could look at us and all of our need and say, "Send them away and let them find their own answer to their need." Instead, He looks on us with compassion. With Jesus's entry into the world, the womb of God has opened up and new possibilities have been born. Salvation and life to the full was made available to all as Mary opened her womb to the compassion of God.

We are invited to respond this way—to see the needs of other people and to take their need as our responsibility. "You feed them," Jesus says to His disciples. I think He is still saying that to us.

SIMPLICITY

▼

Matthew 6:21-34 - "So do not worry, saying, 'What shall we eat?' or 'What shall we drink?' or 'What shall we wear?' For the pagans run after all these things, and your heavenly Father knows that you need them. But seek first his kingdom and his righteousness, and all these things will be given to you as well. Therefore do not worry about tomorrow, for tomorrow will worry about itself. Each day has enough trouble of its own."

Simplicity is about seeking first the Kingdom of Heaven. We don't have to add things to our lives because we have Jesus! Here's your challenge for today: Don't buy something. It could be a candy bar or a sofa. Either way, the challenge is to seek first the Kingdom and remember that you don't need extra stuff.

1. Can you share a story of when another person had compassion on you? What about when God had compassion on you?
2. Can you share a story of when you had compassion on someone else? What did that feel like?
3. How is compassion different from pity?
4. How does it change your understanding of compassion to view it as taking place in the womb of God? What kind of things are "born" out of God's compassion?
5. Who are the people that are moving you to compassion right now? What is God inviting you to do about it?

Read Matthew 9:35-38, Matthew 14:13-16, and reflect on the week.
What has the Holy Spirit revealed to you this week?

SATURDAY | REST

"Are you hurting and broken within?
Overwhelmed by the weight of your sin?
Jesus is calling
Have you come to the end of yourself?
Do you thirst for a drink from the well?

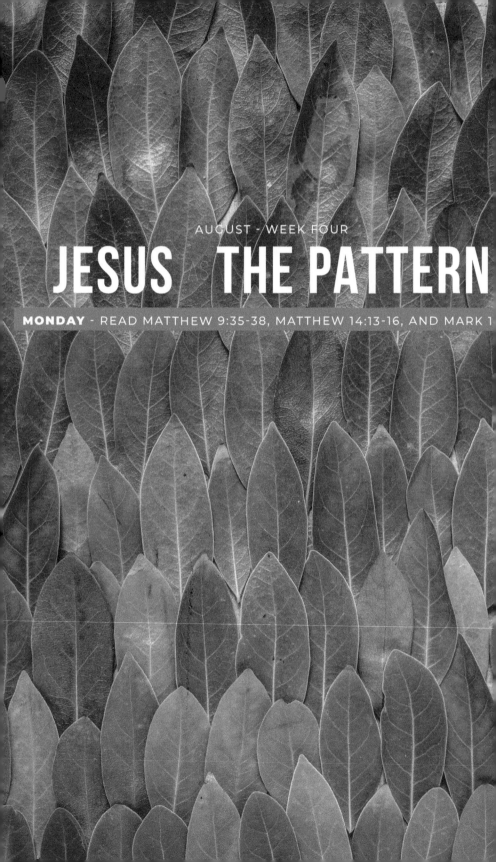

AUGUST - WEEK FOUR

JESUS AS THE PATTERN

MONDAY - READ MATTHEW 9:35-38, MATTHEW 14:13-16, AND MARK 1

When Jesus is moved with compassion, He always does something. Compassion breeds action. But what does Jesus do? The Scriptures for this week are connected. In the first, Jesus sees the multitudes, has compassion on them, and is led to ask His disciples to pray for workers. In the second, Jesus addresses the need by working a miracle—feeding hungry people. The second passage provides a picture of the kinds of workers Jesus is praying for in the first. And in the third, He reminds us that the type of work we do when we break bread and share is our way of showing that we hear Jesus's invitation to us.

In the miracle of Matthew 14, Jesus takes the bread and fish, blesses them, breaks them, and passes them around. The crowd eating that day is numbered at 5000, and that doesn't even include the women and children. Jesus and His disciples are facing a huge need! However, Jesus doesn't ask for the three month's wages it would take to buy them food; He simply asks for the resources available, takes them, blesses them, and passes them around—and it is enough! Often, we refuse to give God what's available because we think it's not enough. But Jesus's first movement is to take what is offered. Have you offered your life to be taken by Jesus? I know, it seems like it's not enough to address all the need in the world. But Jesus doesn't ask for enough; He asks for what's available.

> " Anything plus Jesus—even you or me—is enough. "

When you present yourself to Jesus, He takes that offering. Then, He blesses it. Blessing is putting Himself into the equation. It may look like the fish and bread aren't enough by themselves. It may look like your resources aren't enough and that your skills can't accomplish the task at hand. You're right—they aren't, and they can't! But when Jesus blesses the fish and bread, He adds Himself to the material. Anything plus Jesus—even you or me—is enough.

After He blesses this offering, Jesus breaks it. This is the part that we would rather ignore. But if we are going to be of use, we have to be broken. Brokenness isn't as scary as you think, though. When we are broken, we live in the reality of our need for Jesus. We also live the way Jesus lived: as a broken sacrifice.

Later, in Mark 14, Jesus reclines around a table with His disciples and goes through the same steps. He takes the bread, blesses it, breaks it, and passes it around. What is initially one of Jesus's most astounding miracles becomes a ritual of gratitude aimed at helping His dear friends and followers remember His life, sacrifice, and mission. During this meal, Jesus invites these disciples not only to remember His life but to partake of it: to get it inside of them, to take and eat. He reminds us that He is the bread that will be broken. And as we partake of Him, we are acknowledging His call to be broken as well.

Jesus, then, passes the broken pieces to feed others—the crowd on the mountainside first and His own disciples second. He will also pass us around our world, our church, and our neighborhoods to address the very real needs that surround us.

Taken. Blessed. Broken. Passed around. This is the pattern for a compassionate people of God.

SIMPLICITY

▼

Matthew 6:21-34 - "So do not worry, saying, 'What shall we eat?' or 'What shall we drink?' or 'What shall we wear?' For the pagans run after all these things, and your heavenly Father knows that you need them. But seek first his kingdom and his righteousness, and all these things will be given to you as well. Therefore do not worry about tomorrow, for tomorrow will worry about itself. Each day has enough trouble of its own."

Simplicity is about seeking first the Kingdom of Heaven. We don't have to add things to our lives because we have Jesus! Here's your challenge for today: Don't buy something. It could be a candy bar or a sofa. Either way, the challenge is to seek first the Kingdom and remember that you don't need extra stuff.

1. What does it mean for Jesus to take you? How do you give yourself to Jesus?

2. What does it mean for Jesus to bless you? Have you received this blessing? What does that feel like? How do you receive it?

3. What does it mean for Jesus to break you? Have you experienced this? Can you share a story about it?

4. What does it mean for Jesus to pass you around to the real need that surrounds you? Are you feeling "passed around" to anywhere in particular? Where?

Read Matthew 9:35-38, Matthew 14:13-16, Mark 14:22, and reflect on the week.

What has the Holy Spirit revealed to you this week?

SATURDAY | REST

"This is what the LORD says: "Stand at the crossroads and look; ask for the ancient paths, ask where the good way is, and walk in it, and you will find rest for your souls."
Jeremiah 6:16

SEPTEMBER - WEEK ONE

JESUS AS PROPHET

MONDAY - READ MATTHEW 5:1-20

When we call Jesus a prophet, people usually think that we are saying that He knows the future and can make predictions about what is going to happen, like some sort of fortune teller. But in Scripture, that is not the primary role of a prophet. This vocation has a long history with the people of God and includes two basic functions: 1) Speaking for God to the people and 2) Being a voice for the voiceless (the oppressed, disenfranchised, and poor). This vocation arose during the time of Israel's monarchy, as God used certain people to speak truth to the powerful people and systems that were developing in that monarchy. These people were called prophets and they were usually confrontational! They spoke out against the errors of their own time and they helped us be ready to hear the call of Jesus in the New Testament.

In our passage of Scripture, Jesus is speaking to a crowd on a mountainside and doing just what the Old Testament prophets did: confronting and correcting. His first corrective is simply the fact that He's there, honoring an ordinary group of people with His teaching. The people in power and the religious elite usually leave out the "crowd" and marginalize the masses, but here on the mountainside, we see Jesus speaking to the "crowd" and calling them blessed! He announces that the Kingdom of God and the blessing that comes with it have truly come to everyone, including the group of rag-tag nobodies that are listening to Him. He even calls this crowd the "salt of the earth!"

> " He announces that the Kingdom of God and the blessing that comes with it have truly come to everyone. "

His second correction is in the teaching itself—in His declaration that these ordinary people are the salt of the earth. What does this mean? During Jesus's day, salt had a number of uses. It aided in the preservation of meat and enhanced the taste of food. All by itself, without any processing or special packaging, salt was valuable. When Jesus calls that crowd salt, He is saying they are worthy and ready to be put to use just the way they are. This would have offended the religious elite. If anyone was valuable, they thought, it was those like themselves, with all their education, refined manners, and elaborate rituals—surely not a bunch of underwhelming fishermen and farmers!

To hear another aspect of His prophetic message on the mountain, you should know about another use of salt in Jesus's time. It was often mixed with dried animal droppings to create a common fuel. After many uses, the salt lost the qualities that made it effective in helping this fuel burn longer and hotter. So when it was no longer fit for being mixed with manure, the "saltless" salt was thrown out. The crowd on the mountain, Jesus said, is like that salt—when mixed with lesser, more "earthy" things, they help create long-lasting warmth and light. Yet in this call there is also a caution.

As believers, we receive a challenging call to "mix" with the world yet remain Christian. We must season the world and preserve it against decay. And as we do this, we will burn brightly and create warmth that helps those around. But to do this well, we must claim first and only our identity as members of Christ's family; we must remember that we are with Jesus rather than culture. We must not lose our witness by absorbing the values of the pagan world around us, and neither should we seek to isolate ourselves from unbelievers.

Jesus is not afraid of confrontation! Like a good prophet, He elevates the masses by including them in the Kingdom and speaks for God the Father by calling Israel to bear faithful witness to Him.

SILENCE

Psalm 38:14-15 - "I have become like one who does not hear, whose mouth can offer no reply. Lord, I wait for you; you will answer, Lord my God."

Your silence is a natural part of a conversation. It is allowing the other person to speak. When we are silent with God, we are giving God the space to speak to us. This may be difficult for you. So here is a tip. Choose a word like "Jesus" or "mercy" and every time you feel your mind wandering in your silence, simply whisper your focus word and use it as a call to pay attention to God again. Try to be silent with God for 10 minutes today.

▼

1. What comes to mind when you hear the word "prophet"? Why?

2. In the commentary, we saw that salt is valuable, useful, and mixed in with manure. Which one of these aspects of being salt is the most challenging for you to live out? Why?

3. Have you ever been confronted by Jesus? What is confrontation from Jesus like? How is this related to conviction?

4. If you haven't been confronted by Jesus in a while, why do you think that is?

Read Matthew 5:1-20 and reflect on the week.
What has the Holy Spirit revealed to you this week?

▼

SATURDAY | REST

*"The Lord will fight for you, you
need only to be still." - Exodus 14:14*

SEPTEMBER - WEEK TWO

JESUS AS TEACHER

MONDAY - READ MATTHEW 5:21-48

f I told you that you could learn how to play basketball from anyone in the world, past or present, whom would you pick as your teacher? Chances are, you would pick someone great: someone who has demonstrated their ability to play (or maybe coach) basketball better than anyone else. How would you expect to learn to play basketball if you had LeBron James or John Wooden or Diana Taurasi as your teacher? Would you take notes as you listen to lectures with a PowerPoint? Would you study for multiple-choice quizzes? Of course, there is some information you would have to know in order to learn how to play basketball. You would have to learn the names of the positions, the rules of play, and the vocabulary of the game. But all of this information would be in service of playing the game, and most of your learning would be on the court.

" He has mastered the art of living, and if we listen to His instruction, we can live like Him. "

This is how we should approach hearing from Jesus as our teacher. He has mastered the art of living, and if we listen to His instruction, we can live like Him. As a first step, then, we must admit that He is better at living than we are. In fact, we should pick Jesus as our teacher in life because He is better at living than anyone in history. Sure, there is some information we are going to have to know, such as details in the stories He uses to teach us, or the words of the Lord's prayer. But the information is in service of living like Jesus!

In the Sermon on the Mount, Jesus teaches us about life. This sermon is about how to live in step with God in the same way Jesus did. Another word for that concept is "righteousness." Here is a brief overview of Jesus's teaching from Dallas Willard's "Divine Conspiracy":[9]

Situation	Old Guidelines for Righteousness	Jesus's Guidelines for Righteousness
Irritation with Others	No Murder	No anger/Contempt; Intense desire to be of help
Sexual Attraction	No Adultery	No Cultivation of Lust
Unhappiness with Marriage Partner	If you divorce, give a "pink slip"	No Divorce, as then practiced
Wanting someone to believe something	Keep vows or oaths made to convince	Only say how things are or are not; no verbal manipulation
Being personally injured	Inflict exactly the same injury on the offender	Don't harm but help the one who has hurt you
Having an enemy	Hate your enemy	Love and bless your enemy as your Heavenly Father does

Teaching is often seen as an enterprise of imparting information—getting a set of facts from the teacher's head to the student's. Teachers pour information into their students, like tea into a mug. Then, on exam day, students repeat that information back to prove they have understood it. But in Jesus's day, the main goal of teaching wasn't to dispense information that could be regurgitated on a test but rather to show people how to live differently. In other words, Jesus's main teaching goal was transformation rather than information. The point of this sermon isn't to know what Jesus knows but to live how Jesus lived.

---

[9] Dallas Willard, The Divine Conspiracy (New York. NY: HarperSanFrancisco, 1998); 146

SILENCE

▼

Psalm 38:14-15 - "I have become like one who does not hear, whose mouth can offer no reply. Lord, I wait for you; you will answer, Lord my God."

Your silence is a natural part of a conversation. It is allowing the other person to speak. When we are silent with God, we are giving God the space to speak to us. This may be difficult for you. So here is a tip. Choose a word like "Jesus" or "mercy" and every time you feel your mind wandering in your silence, simply whisper your focus word and use it as a call to pay attention to God again. Try to be silent with God for 10 minutes today.

▼

1. Have you ever thought of Jesus as the smartest person in the world? Why/Why not?

2. What does it mean for Jesus to be the best at living?

3. After Jesus gives a difficult teaching in John 6:53-69, Peter and the twelve refuse to leave him. Why? Have you come to the same conclusions about Jesus and, therefore, won't leave when He teaches something difficult?

4. Is there something difficult that Jesus is teaching you now? What is it? How would believing that He is better at living than you are help you to accept this teaching?

Read Matthew 5:21-48 and reflect on the week.
What has the Holy Spirit revealed to you this week?

SATURDAY | REST

"Be still and know that I am God." Psalm 46:10

SEPTEMBER - WEEK THREE

JESUS AS A DIVIDING FORCE

MONDAY - READ MATTHEW 10:32-39

As we have seen over and over again, life with Jesus is immensely rewarding: You get to learn the best way to live from the greatest teacher, and you see the fruits of your learning in a world reborn. That's something to celebrate. But this comes at a cost: We have to be willing to surrender everything, to be broken, and to obey even when it's hard. One of the ways in which the Christian life proves difficult is in the choices it forces us to make: To be for Jesus is to be against other things. Jesus doesn't make a secret of this. Yes, He came to bring Shalom, but the way to that is rife with conflict. Jesus didn't come to bring peace but a sword.

What does this mean? Let's take an example. A good way to bring some division to a family gathering is to bring up politics. These ideas have the power to separate (usually along party lines) because of people's allegiance to them. Sometimes, people choose loyalty to a party platform over a family member. This reality highlights the fact that we are very familiar with forces that divide. Could Jesus be one of these forces?

A sword is usually thought of as an instrument of destruction or murder. But Jesus is not saying that He came to kill and destroy. In fact, we are told in no uncertain terms that it is our enemy who comes to steal, kill, and destroy while Jesus comes to give life (John 10:10). When He says that He came to bring the sword, Jesus instead conjured up prophetic images of the Day of the Lord. In the Jewish tradition, God's judgment is often spoken of as a sword, and the Day of the Lord is described as a dark, distressing time in which the righteous are separated from the unrighteous, the people of God from the people of the world. The sword here acts as an instrument of separation rather than an instrument of death. Mothers may be separated from daughters and fathers from sons, not because of violence but because they have different allegiances.

It is true that Jesus came to bring peace between God and man. But to enjoy this peace, we must give Jesus our full allegiance. We may have to choose between peace with God and acceptance from other people. Like a sword, Jesus cuts our lives in two: Him and not Him. When we are called to choose, Jesus's expectation is clear. We are to choose Him. Jesus or family? Jesus. Jesus or political party? Jesus. Jesus or job security? Jesus. Jesus or friends? Jesus. May there be no competing allegiances. All Jesus. Only Jesus.

SILENCE

▼

Psalm 38:14-15 - "I have become like one who does not hear, whose mouth can offer no reply. Lord, I wait for you; you will answer, Lord my God."

Your silence is a natural part of a conversation. It is allowing the other person to speak. When we are silent with God, we are giving God the space to speak to us. This may be difficult for you. So here is a tip. Choose a word like "Jesus" or "mercy" and every time you feel your mind wandering in your silence, simply whisper your focus word and use it as a call to pay attention to God again. Try to be silent with God for 10 minutes today.

▼

1. Why do you think the Day of the Lord had a connotation of being darkness and gloom?
2. Describe a time when choosing Jesus cost you a relationship (or a promotion or success).
3. Why does Jesus ask for our full allegiance?
4. Are there any competing allegiances in your heart? What are they? How can you rectify this?

....

....

....

....

....

....

....

....

....

....

....

....

Read Matthew 10:32-39 and reflect on the week.
What has the Holy Spirit revealed to you this week?

SATURDAY | REST

*"Come to me, all you who are weary and burdened,
and I will give you rest." Matthew 11:28*

SEPTEMBER - WEEK FOUR

JESUS WHAT WE NEED

MONDAY - READ JOHN 6:25-66

The focus of this month has been on the hard teachings of Jesus—that sometimes following Jesus means confronting cultural values or holding an unpopular opinion, that learning from Jesus is a long and costly undertaking, and that sometimes our allegiance to Jesus will cost us friends or earthly means of security. This week's teaching is so hard that it causes most of the people following Him to turn away (vs. 66). What was it about this teaching that made it so difficult?

First, we need to recall that the crowd that was following Jesus had mixed motives. If you read the beginning of the chapter, you'll recall that this is the same crowd of 5000 that Jesus had miraculously fed with five loaves of bread and two fish. They had their fill that day, and Jesus was happy to feed them. However, that bread didn't sustain forever. So there they are, waiting on the other side of the lake with empty stomachs, expecting Jesus to do it again. Jesus sees their motivation and refuses to give them what they are looking for.

> " Often, Jesus won't give us what we're looking for because we're looking for the wrong thing. "

Often, Jesus won't give us what we're looking for because we're looking for the wrong thing. Jesus calls the crowd out on just this error, saying they seek Him only for the earthly food He can provide—but then He turns the tables, inviting them to seek instead the bread of everlasting life. Jesus issues a clear call: Come to Him, the bread of life, and never be hungry again. The crowd understands Jesus's message and who He is claiming to be; they just don't believe Him. "How can He come down from heaven?" they ask. They think they know Jesus—He's just a local kid with parents named Mary and Joseph—so they refuse to believe He has anything important to say to them.

This teaching is also hard because it requires the crowd to read beyond the surface. The crowd in this story sees a miracle but misses the sign within it—that the bread and fish Jesus offers them is only the beginning of how He can feed their needs. A sign, you may have guessed, is something that points beyond the physical, concrete meaning to reveal something deeper. In this case, the sign of the bread and fish reveals something about who Jesus is. By looking past the sign, this crowd misses Jesus.

In this teaching, Jesus links Himself with the miraculous manna in the wilderness as well as with the bread He provided on the hillside a few verses earlier. Manna is not the bread of life, but it points to God's provision for the world that would come later. Jesus is the culmination of that Old Testament sign, the true bread of life provided by God for the salvation of man. Only when we partake in the meal He shares—His broken body and poured out blood—can we participate in His work. This teaching is simply too hard for the crowd, who can't think beyond the literal level of their own physical hunger. Eat flesh? Drink blood? No.

So they make a sad choice, leaving Jesus to get food. They seek the things of the earth and want the things of heaven to be added to them, when really, Jesus teaches it the other way around (Matthew 6:33).

As finite beings, it is all too easy to focus on the material things we need to sustain us. We think the basic things of life are things like bread, water, clothing, and shelter. What if there is a more basic human need? What if Jesus is really what sustains us?

SILENCE

▼

Psalm 38:14-15 - "I have become like one who does not hear, whose mouth can offer no reply. Lord, I wait for you; you will answer, Lord my God."

Your silence is a natural part of a conversation. It is allowing the other person to speak. When we are silent with God, we are giving God the space to speak to us. This may be difficult for you. So here is a tip. Choose a word like "Jesus" or "mercy" and every time you feel your mind wandering in your silence, simply whisper your focus word and use it as a call to pay attention to God again. Try to be silent with God for 10 minutes today.

▼

1. What are the material things you would sacrifice Jesus to obtain because you think you need them? (Be honest.)
2. How might the manna in the wilderness and the bread in the feeding of the 5000 reveal who Jesus is?
3. What does it mean to follow Jesus with mixed motives?
4. What are some things Jesus said that you don't believe all the way?
5. Read John 4:32. What "bread" do you think Jesus was speaking of here?

Read John 6:25-66 and reflect on the week.
What has the Holy Spirit revealed to you this week?

▼

SATURDAY | REST

"Come with me by yourselves to a quiet place and get some rest." Mark 6:31b

OCTOBER - WEEK ONE

JESUS AS GENEROUS

MONDAY - READ JOHN 3:16 AND PSALM 34:8-10

During the past nine months, we have learned to see, live, and hear Jesus better. All of this prepares us to do what Jesus says is the chief commandment: to love God. The better we know Jesus, the easier that is to do! Let's finish out this last quarter of the year by thinking through some ways that we can love God better.

One of the great blessings of getting to know and love Jesus better is to discover and meditate on His goodness. The psalmist invites us to discover this for ourselves: "Taste and see that the Lord is good. Oh, the joys of those who take refuge in him!" (34:8). One of the practical ways we can taste the goodness of God is through His enormous generosity.

I was reminded of God's generosity recently by my youngest son. After I bought him a coffee, he immediately wanted to share it with me. I said, "No thanks. I bought that for you, son." His response was wonderful: "I know, but I want to return the favor and share it with you." This was just a simple, ordinary event. But let me explain how it reminded me of God's generosity.

> " Taste and see that the Lord is good. Oh, the joys of those who take refuge in him! "

My son wasn't sharing anything that wasn't first given to him. It fills my heart with gratitude to remember all the things my Heavenly Father has given me. If there is anything I have to give, it is because I have been given so much! I saw this take shape in my son that day. It was out of his gratitude that he was able to be generous. Ultimately, my son offered me some of that coffee because he was sure that it wouldn't be the last coffee that I would purchase for him. His generosity came from a confidence in my generosity. The same is true with our Heavenly Father.

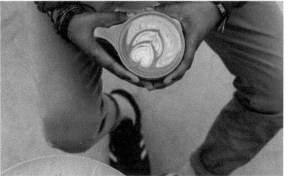

Jesus was confident that His heavenly Father wasn't holding out on Him. As a result, He was able to give His own life away freely, certain that He would not be able to out-give His Father. Likewise, I can be ready to give Jesus anything He asks for out of an understanding that what I have to give wasn't mine to begin with: it was given to me.

The older I get, the more I discover that I can't really possess anything. I just need to make sure that nothing other than God's Spirit possesses me. When I live understanding the goodness of Jesus and His provision in my life, I discover what means to live free.

After penning this commentary, I am headed to the store to purchase yet another coffee drink for my son. His generosity has actually made me want to be more generous. As I go, I can't help but marvel at what Jesus has so generously given to me and you. May we be willing to give as freely as He.

GENEROSITY

▼

2 Corinthians 9:6 - "Remember this: Whoever sows sparingly will also reap sparingly, and whoever sows generously will also reap generously."

Generosity is close to the heart of God who loved the world so much that He gave his only son. Give a gift to someone today.

▼

1. What is the significance of God "giving" His son in John 3:16?

2. Where in Scripture do you see Jesus being generous to the people around Him? What does the generosity of His Heavenly Father have to do with Jesus's generosity?

3. How have you personally experienced the generosity of Jesus?

4. How does the generosity of Jesus inspire you to be more generous in your own life?

....

....

....

....

....

....

....

....

....

....

....

....

....

Read John 3:16, Psalm 34:8-10, and reflect on the week.
What has the Holy Spirit revealed to you this week?

SATURDAY | REST

*"In peace I will lie down and sleep, for
you alone, Lord, make me dwell in safety."*
Psalm 4:8

OCTOBER - WEEK TWO

JESUS AS OUR FIRST LOVE

MONDAY - READ MARK 12:13-17 AND REVELATION 2:1-7

We've said this before, but it bears repeating: We are owned by what we love. Do you remember the game called "Hungry, Hungry, Hippos?" In this game, the players all pound a lever, which controls the head of a hippo. The goal is to get your hippo to scoop up and "eat" more marbles than everyone else in the game. It is a fun game to play. However, we can often feel like the marbles—bouncing around the middle while outside forces compete for our attention and grab for us in an effort to own us.

Today's passage includes a question that exposes the various forces that are seeking to own God's people. After Rome conquered an area, they usually imposed a heavy tax burden, which served to underscore their ownership of that area. With their question about taxes, the Pharisees and Herodians are trying to force Jesus into a debate on ownership—Is it right for Israel to be owned by Rome? If Jesus answers "yes, you should pay taxes," then people in the crowd will shake their fists at Him, taking Him for a Roman sympathizer who clearly doesn't understand the depth of oppression and heartache Rome inflicts on Israel. If He answers "no," then another section of the crowd will shake their heads at Him—a zealot who doesn't seem to understand the cost that would be paid in blood in a war with Rome. This question has serious political, economic, and religious overtones. No matter what He answers, Jesus will upset somebody. It's a perfect setup: That's why the Pharisees and Herodians ask Him the question. But Jesus uses the opportunity to teach them a deeper lesson.

Jesus points to the picture of Caesar on a Roman coin and asks, "Whose image is this?" Now it's Jesus's turn for a loaded question. In the Jewish story, it is human beings who bear the image of God. Furthermore, as they know very well, the Jewish people aren't supposed to make for themselves any graven images. Jesus might be asking, "Do you have an idol in your pocket?" Caesar is making a claim of ownership on the coins by marking them with his image. So what does it mean for God to mark humans with His image? Giving to Caesar what belongs to Caesar means letting go of our money idol. Giving to God what belongs to God means giving Him our very selves. Jesus uses a question about taxes as an opportunity to remind everyone listening that God is laying claim to them and desires that they be owned by Him.

When we hear Jesus telling us to give everything to God—that God has laid claim to our very lives—we tend to hear it as a harsh command by a jealous God rather than an invitation to love. However, Jesus knows that other owners will ravage us. Our families, financial planners, political parties, jobs, and churches are all making their claims of ownership on our lives. There's one reason to choose Jesus: He's better. When He is our first love, those other things can find their proper place. They can't own us because we are already claimed.

GENEROSITY

▼

2 Corinthians 9:6 - "Remember this: Whoever sows sparingly will also reap sparingly, and whoever sows generously will also reap generously."

Generosity is close to the heart of God who loved the world so much that He gave his only son. Give a gift to someone today.

▼

1. Name some examples of things competing for your attention and allegiance (family vs. work, etc).

2. Look at your bank statement. According to how you spend your money, what is your highest priority? Are your priorities in alignment with your desire to follow Jesus?

3. Look at your calendar. According to how you spend your time, what is your highest priority? Are your priorities in alignment with your desire to follow Jesus?

4. What does it mean to make something an idol? How do these things own you?

5. Why do you believe that Jesus wants you to let go of these idols?

6. What do you have to surrender in order to recover Jesus as your first love?

....

....

....

....

....

....

....

....

....

Read Mark 12:13-17, Revelation 2:1-7, and reflect on the week.
What has the Holy Spirit revealed to you this week?

▼

SATURDAY | REST

*"Take my yoke upon you and learn from
me, for I am gentle and humble in heart,
and you will find rest for your souls."*
Matthew 11:29

JESUS CHEERLEADER

MONDAY - READ LUKE 21:1-4 AND HEBREWS 12:1-3

I have played competitive sports for most of my life. For the most part, if it bounces, I enjoy it. During my childhood, my dad seldom came to any of my games—as a fisherman desperate to feed his family, he spent more time in the Atlantic Ocean than he did on solid ground. As a father of three myself, I have attempted to make up for lost time by attending all of my kids' sporting events. As they've competed over the years, they've always looked up into the stands to make sure I was watching. Honestly, I think much of their motivation was simply to make me proud. It matters when we have a cheerleader; it motivates us to do our very best.

In Mark's and Luke's Gospels we see the most unsuspecting widow woman catch the attention of Jesus. There is no doubt that this poor woman might as well have been invisible in the midst of all the people in the temple that day. In fact, she probably didn't want to be seen, since her offering seemed meager in comparison to all the others. As Jesus watches her walk toward the offering box, though, He quickly gets the attention of His disciples so He can make her one of the greatest case studies of generosity the world would ever know. Jesus points to her and proclaims, "I tell you the truth...this poor widow has given more than all the rest of them. For they have given a tiny part of their surplus, but she, poor as she is, has given everything she has" (Luke 21:3-4).

I just love this. The widow woman has no idea that Jesus, the Son of God, is sitting in the stands and cheering on her generosity. I'm not sure how many millionaires brought their offerings that morning, but none of them is singled out by Jesus. Why? Generosity isn't measured by the size of your gift but rather by the size of your sacrifice. The depth of the sacrifice has always been more important than the amount you offer.

How much has Jesus given you? Do you know that generosity is measured in the sacrifice? This should invite you to think about just how generous Jesus has been because He sacrificed all of Himself for you. He held nothing back. We are being cheered on by Goodness Himself.

If you have been given much, make sure you never forget that much more will be required. Jesus is pulling for you to be joyfully generous because He was and it's the best possible way to live. After laying down His life, hear Him cheering for you to do the same: "You can do it!"

GENEROSITY

2 Corinthians 9:6 - "Remember this: Whoever sows sparingly will also reap sparingly, and whoever sows generously will also reap generously."

Generosity is close to the heart of God who loved the world so much that He gave his only son. Give a gift to someone today.

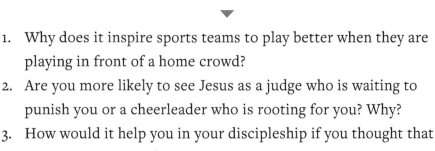

1. Why does it inspire sports teams to play better when they are playing in front of a home crowd?
2. Are you more likely to see Jesus as a judge who is waiting to punish you or a cheerleader who is rooting for you? Why?
3. How would it help you in your discipleship if you thought that Jesus was cheering for you?
4. What is one tangible way you can celebrate the generosity of someone else this week?

Read Luke 21:1-4, Hebrews 12:1-3, and reflect on the week.
What has the Holy Spirit revealed to you this week?

SATURDAY | REST

"I said, 'Oh, that I had the wings of a dove! I would fly away and be at rest.'" Psalm 55:6

OCTOBER - WEEK FOUR

JESUS AS BEAUTIFUL

MONDAY - READ LUKE 21:1-4 AND HEBREWS 12:1-3

When I was in middle school, my family lived in Germany for a while. One of the more memorable things about my time in Europe was visiting old cathedrals. Just about every village had a large church right in the middle of it. Sometimes the churches were in ruins or abandoned. But most of the time, the structure was still there—a giant of a building towering over the village. I used to love these places because I could imagine the church bells ringing out over the small town calling people to worship. When you entered these churches, everything was quieter. Tourists would saunter in with a drink in their hands laughing and looking back at the stragglers making their way through the door. But as soon as they turned around, they would be hushed in a sense of wonder and awe. The ceilings could swallow you up. The carvings and stained glass called for your attention and reminded you that people worked hard to set this place apart. I remember feeling their sacredness and wanting to walk quieter and slower in these churches. They were beautiful and made you feel as though you were entering a holy place, a place set apart for God.

I imagine this is the sense of awe the disciples felt that day as they were pointing out the beauty of the temple to Jesus. Given that, His response is a bit jarring: One day, He says, this beauty will be destroyed; it isn't an eternal beauty. Wait—doesn't Jesus appreciate the temple? This might seem to be a strange comment unless we see it through a different lens.

Earlier, Jesus refers to Himself as the temple of God. He participates in baptisms that take place away from the temple. The Jesus-movement invites people into a post-temple world where the Kingdom of God is at hand and not relegated to the temple's space. So the destruction of the temple has a double meaning: 1) The temple as Jesus's body will be crucified and 2) The temple as the building where God lives will be abandoned as God makes His home within His people. It is not that Jesus doesn't appreciate the temple but that He wants to spread the goodness of God's sacred presence to the hearts of all His followers.

As the disciples are admiring the stones of the temple, Jesus is pointing to the cross. It is almost as if He is saying, "You think this is beautiful? You haven't seen anything yet!" He is right. The carved stones and decorations, beautiful though they may be, are but the palest reflection of the beauty we see in the picture of Jesus taking the full force of sin and death for the sake of His love. Come and admire the beauty of the cross. Let it silence you in awe as you gaze into the very heart of Christ.

GENEROSITY

▼

2 Corinthians 9:6 - "Remember this: Whoever sows sparingly will also reap sparingly, and whoever sows generously will also reap generously."

Generosity is close to the heart of God who loved the world so much that He gave his only son. Give a gift to someone today.

▼

1. What changes in you when you enter a beautiful location?
2. Why does beauty have such an impact on us?
3. Do you think of the cross as beautiful? Why/Why not?
4. What would change in your prayer life if you spent some time every day contemplating the cross?

Read Luke 21:5-6, John 2:13-22, and reflect on the week.
What has the Holy Spirit revealed to you this week?

SATURDAY | REST

"Whenever Jesus comes he establishes rest..."
Oswald Chambers

NOVEMBER - WEEK ONE

JESUS HEALER

MONDAY - READ JOHN 5:1-8

This month, we are focusing on a set of stories that can help us love Jesus better—miracles. I don't know if you've ever seen a miracle occur—and they still do—but I know that in all cases, they're meant to draw us closer to God, to help us to see His rhythms so we can walk in step with them.

"Walking with God" is a common phrase in the Scriptures. Adam and Eve, Enoch, Noah, Abraham, Isaac, and Jacob are all said to have walked with God. The phrase connotes a sense of relationship or union—a moving beside and in step with God. Early in humanity's story, sin disrupts our ability to walk with God. After Adam and Eve sin, they stop walking with God and instead go into hiding. So when Jesus approaches a lame man—one who cannot walk at all—at the sheep gate, the encounter is dripping with symbolism and expectation. Jesus asks the man if he wants to get well. The man doesn't even answer the question but instead starts offering excuses. I think we have the same excuses about why we don't want to get well and walk with God.

First excuse: He believes that a power other than Jesus should heal him. Some versions include a commentary about the pool next to which this man is lying. The thinking at the time was that an angel would descend into the pool and stir the waters, at which point the first person who got in the stirred water would be healed. This paralyzed man has God right in front of him, but he fixates instead on the power of a mysterious pool. I think we too can fixate on some kind of experience rather than on a relationship with God. We think something like this: "I'll walk with God if He [heals my mother/delivers me from my addiction/saves my son/makes me emotional during a worship song...]" Fill in the blank with whatever you desire most. No matter how you fill it in, the point is that sometimes we're seeking an experience to help us feel better rather than a relationship with the true Healer.

Second excuse: He blames other people. The lame man says, "No one will help me into the pool." The man sees his brokenness as other people's fault; he believes he's in a bad situation because of what others have not done for him. Sometimes Jesus asks us if we want to be healed, but instead of accepting the healing He offers, all we see is how other people have hurt us.

Third excuse: He doesn't see himself as worthy of healing. Looking around, the man sees all these other people being healed while he sits there paralyzed. "Someone always beats me to it," he says.

This plays out in our own lives when we start to think things like this: "It's just my lot to get close enough to see the miracle in other people's lives but not to experience it on my own" or "I'm too broken to be made well." When we fall into that pattern, we start to believe that our condition is too dirty or too broken for God to want to share, and we see other people as more "worthy" of a miracle.

Into all of these excuses (the lame man's and ours), Jesus speaks: Get up. Start Walking. Be Healed. But the question He asks first is one for us as well: "Do you want to get well?"

GRATITUDE

▼

Colossians 3:16 - "Let the message of Christ dwell among you richly as you teach and admonish one another with all wisdom through psalms, hymns, and songs from the Spirit, singing to God with gratitude in your hearts."

Gratitude is an expression of worship. Make a list of 25 things for which you are grateful today.

▼

1. Where do you need healing in your life?
2. Why might someone answer "no" to Jesus's question, "Do you want to get well?" What does healing cost?
3. How has the hurt caused by other people in your life hindered your walk with Jesus?
4. How does shame keep us from walking with Jesus?
5. What in your past is producing shame for you? How do you overcome this shame?

Read John 5:1-8 and reflect on the week.
What has the Holy Spirit revealed to you this week?

▼

SATURDAY | REST

*"The Lord is my shepherd, I lack nothing. He
makes me lie down in green pastures, he leads
me beside quiet waters, he refreshes my soul."*
Psalm 23:1-3

NOVEMBER - WEEK TWO

JESUS AS THE FINGER OF GOD

MONDAY - READ LUKE 11:14-22, EXODUS 8:19, AND EXODUS 31:18

The phrase Jesus uses here, "the finger of God," has a rich history with the people of God and is linked to some of the most defining moments in Israel's history. When we see this phrase, we know that God is about to act with great power and authority.

When Moses goes to Pharaoh, God instructs him to perform various signs to prove that he has been sent from God. However, Pharaoh's magicians are able to perform these signs as well, so Pharaoh's heart is hardened. The first time "the finger of God" is used, it actually comes out of the mouth of Pharaoh's magicians! It happens when they are unable to perform a miracle that Moses and Aaron perform. They look at Pharaoh and proclaim, "This is the finger of God."

Then, after Israel is released from Egyptian bondage, they travel through the wilderness where God leads them to a mountain. He makes a covenant with them and gives them a list of rules that are meant to fashion them into His people for the purpose of making a holy nation. These rules are the 10 Commandments and were written by...the finger of God.

As we can see, this phrase is linked both with the plagues that led to Israel's freedom and with the covenant that showed they belonged to God. The finger of God points God's people out of slavery to a dark kingdom and directs them into His Kingdom instead. No wonder Jesus says He uses the finger of God to free a man from demonic possession!

When a person is possessed by a demon, there is a power that holds him in its grip and refuses to free him; it forces that person to do things he wouldn't do unless he were bound by it. With this in mind, perhaps we could think of a demon as an echo of Egypt. When Jesus drives out demons, He is probing—inserting the finger of God— into this personal oppression and proving that He is stronger than the power that binds. He demonstrates that He has the authority to rescue people from the power of darkness and to point to them as His own.

We may not speak much about demon possession anymore. But perhaps the evils of other "Egypts" have a grip on you: power, money, sex, etc. Jesus has the ability to free you from these powers and to bring you into the Kingdom of God.

GRATITUDE

▼

Colossians 3:16 - "Let the message of Christ dwell among you richly as you teach and admonish one another with all wisdom through psalms, hymns, and songs from the Spirit, singing to God with gratitude in your hearts."

Gratitude is an expression of worship. Make a list of 25 things for which you are grateful today.

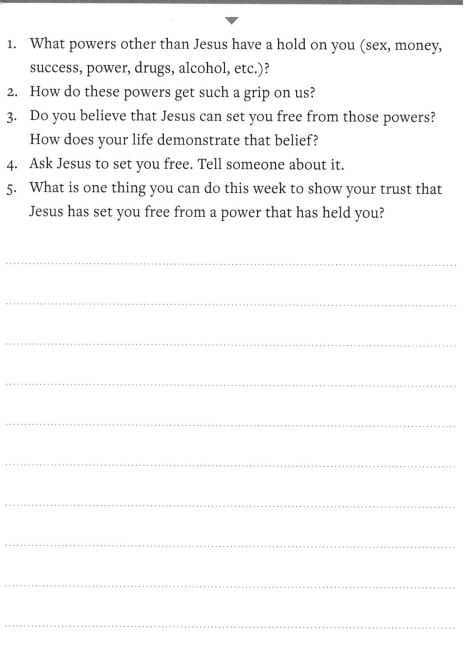

1. What powers other than Jesus have a hold on you (sex, money, success, power, drugs, alcohol, etc.)?
2. How do these powers get such a grip on us?
3. Do you believe that Jesus can set you free from those powers? How does your life demonstrate that belief?
4. Ask Jesus to set you free. Tell someone about it.
5. What is one thing you can do this week to show your trust that Jesus has set you free from a power that has held you?

Read Luke 11:14-22, Exodus 8:19, Exodus 31:18, and reflect on the week.
What has the Holy Spirit revealed to you this week?

▼

SATURDAY | REST

*Peace I leave with you; my peace I give you. I
do not give to you as the world gives. Do not let
your hearts be troubled and do not be afraid.*

John 14:27

JESUS AS THE GOSPEL

MONDAY - READ LUKE 4:16-19 AND MARK 5:1-20

In the beginning of His ministry, Jesus announces the year of the Lord's favor. He declares that He is anointed to proclaim good news for the poor, freedom for the prisoner, and sight for the blind. All of Jesus's miracles underscore that main mission. This week, we are looking at how this good news (or gospel) is displayed in the life of one man in a graveyard.

If ever a person needed some good news, this man does. As the story begins, he is in a very bad place, oppressed and held captive by demons. As a result, society has banished him to live among the tombs, where he can be heard crying out at night and harming himself. Talk about a tortured man! He is alone, left to destroy himself. But Jesus enters his life and sets him free, and the demons that had lived in him have to go reside instead in a herd of pigs.

The reaction of the village is alarming: They are angry and ask Jesus to leave. Apparently they value a herd of pigs more than this man's life! Not surprisingly, this man wants to go with Jesus. He has experienced the Gospel that Jesus came to announce, and as a result, he loves Him. Rather than inviting him to come along, however, Jesus sends him back to his own people as a representative of the Gospel. So the man goes home to the Gerasenes, in the region of the Decapolis.

He goes on to do just what Jesus asked. How do we know? Well, when Jesus returns to the region some time later, instead of being asked to leave, he is met with a request for a healing (Mark 7:31-32). Eventually, there is a crowd of 4000 men surrounding Jesus, getting healed, and listening to His teaching (Mark 8:1-9).

What changed? Could it be that this demon-possessed man did what Jesus asked him to do? Could he have traveled throughout the region of the Decapolis proclaiming what Jesus had done for him?

The miracles of Jesus are always in service of the gospel. I can't explain why some people get healed and others don't. However, I think we can trust that Jesus is always proclaiming the gospel: the good news that a new King has come for the poor to set the prisoner free, give sight to the blind, and proclaim the year of the Lord's favor. Sometimes that proclamation comes with a miracle. With or without such obvious miracles, though, I pray that the gospel comes to you and that you bring it to those around you.

GRATITUDE

▼

Colossians 3:16 - "Let the message of Christ dwell among you richly as you teach and admonish one another with all wisdom through psalms, hymns, and songs from the Spirit, singing to God with gratitude in your hearts."

Gratitude is an expression of worship. Make a list of 25 things for which you are grateful today.

▼

1. What is the Gospel of Jesus?

2. What changes in how you see the miracles of Jesus if you see them all as signs pointing to the Gospel?

3. What does it mean to want the "signs" of the Gospel without wanting the Gospel?

4. Are there things Jesus has done in your life that you consider miraculous? How might these things be in service of the Gospel?

....

....

....

....

....

....

....

....

....

....

....

....

Read Luke 4:16-19, Mark 5:1-20, and reflect on the week.
What has the Holy Spirit revealed to you this week?

SATURDAY | REST

Jesus knows we must come apart and rest awhile, or else we may just plain come apart." - Vance Havner

NOVEMBER - WEEK FOUR

JESUS AS THE AUTHORITY

MONDAY - READ MARK 4:35-41 AND PSALM 4:8

Water and wind are powerful forces. If you've ever lived in hurricane country, you know what I mean. These storms are so powerful that most places that experience them will have marked hurricane evacuation routes. We all know that these forces are too strong for us and that our only recourse is to run away. And if—God forbid—we ever happen to find ourselves in a situation where we are feeling the brunt force of the wind and waves, most of us will end up feeling like a nervous wreck. By contrast, when He was in a storm, Jesus went to sleep.

Sleep is such a wonderful gift! Yet it seems people are finding it increasingly harder to go to sleep and stay asleep. The sheer amount of sleeping medication available is evidence of it—and there is no prescription that will silence all the alarms going off in our hearts and keeping us from true rest. This pattern is a symptom of a worried and fearful people. Jesus, however, is able to entrust His life to His heavenly Father. The same trust that enables Him to say "not my will but Thine be done" is the trust that allows Him to close his eyes and sleep.

Sleep carries with it a connotation of peace. When we see Jesus sleeping, we are seeing a Jesus at rest. Do you think this is the only time Jesus slept? I'm sure it wasn't. Jesus can rest during a storm or during the calm because His rest isn't contingent upon His circumstances. Jesus wants us to be able to rest as well. I think this is why Jesus asks the disciples hard questions about fear and faith. What do they have to be afraid of? Jesus is with them. Do they not trust that He will take care of them? By calming the wind and the waves, Jesus demonstrates that He has both the authority to speak into our circumstances and the compassion to help when we need it. He may not always calm your storms. But He will always be present, inviting you to trust and be at peace. Indeed, you can rest in His power. We come to love Him more as we rest in Him.

GRATITUDE

▼

Colossians 3:16 - "Let the message of Christ dwell among you richly as you teach and admonish one another with all wisdom through psalms, hymns, and songs from the Spirit, singing to God with gratitude in your hearts."

Gratitude is an expression of worship. Make a list of 25 things for which you are grateful today.

1. Do you have trouble sleeping? Why?
2. Describe a circumstance in your life right now that worries you. Why are you worried about it?
3. Why doesn't God calm EVERY storm?
4. Could the disciples have followed Jesus's lead and slept in the midst of the storm? Why do you think they didn't?
5. What is the relationship between trust and peace?

....

....

....

....

....

....

....

....

....

....

....

....

Read Mark 4:35-41, Psalm 4:8, and reflect on the week.
What has the Holy Spirit revealed to you this week?

SATURDAY | REST

"Truly my soul finds rest in God; my salvation comes from him." Psalm 62:1

DECEMBER - WEEK ONE

JESUS AS THE PROMISED ONE

MONDAY - READ JEREMIAH 33:14-16 AND MATTHEW 24:36-51

The season of Advent takes place around the winter solstice, when the nights are the longest and the darkest. Like a candle on a window sill, Advent draws our attention away from the darkness to the light. We focus on the promise that we have rather than the despair around us.

So, for the next four weeks, you are invited to participate in Advent, which means "coming." Yes, Jesus came. But He is also coming today and will one day return fully in glory. He was, is, and will be present with us. In the midst of the darkest night, we hear the words of the promise.

A promise can give rise to a new hope for the future, which in turn changes how we approach the present. For example, if your family is anything like mine, the promise of someone coming over to your house for dinner will undoubtedly alter your activity leading up to that event. You clean the bathrooms, pick up the living room, cook a nice dinner, and perhaps even complain about those things that need fixing but never get attention. In other words, as you make preparations for the visit, you see your house through a different lens. The promise of Advent should lead us into a similar preparatory posture.

The need for preparation is why all of the Gospels give an account of John the Baptist's ministry before they give an account of Jesus's. It is all too easy for spiritual clutter to build up and for us to ignore those sinful areas of our lives that need to be addressed. Jesus came, Jesus is coming, and Jesus will come again. The promise has been given. Are you ready?

FELLOWSHIP

▼

1 John 1:3 - "We proclaim to you what we have seen and heard, so that you also may have fellowship with us. And our fellowship is with the Father and with his Son, Jesus Christ."

God exists in an eternal relationship: Father, Son, and Holy Spirit. When Christians come together and testify to their life with Jesus, they are joining this fellowship.

Have lunch or coffee with someone today and listen to their story. Ask how you can pray for them and then pray for each other.

1. Why is it important that we celebrate the promise of Advent during the darkest time of the year?

2. What is the darkness you are facing right now? How does the promise of the coming of Jesus bring light to that darkness?

3. What preparations do you need to do in order to receive Jesus into your life this Advent season?

Read Jeremiah 33:14-16, Matthew 24:36-51, and reflect on the week.
What has the Holy Spirit revealed to you this week?

▼

SATURDAY | REST

*"If we dig down a little deeper, we may see that
our unwillingness to practice sabbath is really
an unwillingness to live within the limits of our
humanity, to honor our finiteness. We cling to some
sense that we are indispensable and that the world
cannot go on without us even for a day. Or we feel that
certain tasks and activities are more significant than
the delights that God is wanting to share with us."*
*- Ruth Haley Barton. Sacred Rhythms (InterVarsity
Press, Downers Grove, IL. 2009), 138.*

DECEMBER - WEEK TWO

JESUS AS EMMANUEL

MONDAY - READ MATTHEW 1:18-25

Recently, I heard a children's evangelist proclaim the Gospel using Christmas imagery. One of the first things he spoke about was a Christmas tree and how it is always pointing up to the heavens where God is. This is the mentality that permeates the "good news" that I usually hear: God is somewhere up in the sky, and we should want to leave earth to go be with Him in heaven. However, the Christmas story shows us a picture of God who is with us on earth. We don't have to go anywhere to find Him, He is already here.

With so many demands on our attention, it is easy to forget that God is with us—indeed that God wants to be with us. However, that is the source of hope and joy that drives the Advent season. We hear the promise, and we wait and we watch. In fact, when we stop anticipating the coming of Jesus into our ordinary, broken lives, our hope and joy start to fade. Advent is a time to remember that God is already here and longs to be close. Did you catch that? God wants to be close; not merely closer but close.

So keep this in mind: When you go to the grocery story, God is with you. When you wash the dishes, God is with you. When you drive your kids to school, God is with you. When you mourn the loss of a loved one, welcome the birth of a child, or get cut off in traffic, Emmanuel, God-is-with-you, loving you and drawing you near.

FELLOWSHIP

▼

1 John 1:3 - "We proclaim to you what we have seen and heard, so that you also may have fellowship with us. And our fellowship is with the Father and with his Son, Jesus Christ."

God exists in an eternal relationship: Father, Son, and Holy Spirit. When Christians come together and testify to their life with Jesus, they are joining this fellowship.

Have lunch or coffee with someone today and listen to their story. Ask how you can pray for them and then pray for each other.

▼

1. Have you ever felt the presence of Jesus? Describe those moments.
2. Why is it hard to believe that Jesus is with you always?
3. What are some things you can do to prepare your heart to notice the presence of Jesus?
4. How do you think Joseph felt about the coming of Jesus? How can you relate to the coming of Jesus in your own life?
5. Is the presence of Jesus comforting or challenging? How so?

Read Matthew 1:18-25 and reflect on the week.
What has the Holy Spirit revealed to you this week?

▼

SATURDAY | REST

*"What I do know is there have to be times in your life
when you move slow . . . times when you walk rather
than run, allowing your body to settle into each step
. . . times when you sit and gaze admiringly at loved
ones, rather than racing through an agenda . . . times
when you receive food and drink with gratitude and
humility rather than gulping it down on your way to
something 'more important.' Times when hugs linger
and kisses are real."*

- *Ruth Haley Barton. Sacred Rhythms*
(InterVarsity Press, Downers Grove, IL. 2009), 144.

DECEMBER - WEEK THREE

JESUS AS THE NAZARENE

MONDAY - READ LUKE 1:26-38 AND MATTHEW 25:31-40

In today's passage, we learn that Mary is a peasant girl. According to the way our world works, she isn't supposed to be a highly favored person in the eyes of God. She isn't a priest who is cleaned up and chosen to enter the holy of holies. She isn't a part of a powerful family with inroads to the religious elite. No, she is from a poor family in the obscure town of Nazareth on the edge of the kingdom. People can't imagine anything good coming from Nazareth. Yet God chooses Mary to carry His Son, thereby flipping the standard of what it means to be "blessed" upside down.

All of a sudden, the normal, forgotten people of the world are blessed. Jesus shocks the religious leaders during His day with an inclusive message of God's love. Steve Chalke highlights this: "Jesus demonstrates love and redemption as he embraces the untouchable, feeds the hungry, eats with the socially and religiously unacceptable, forgives the unforgivable, heals the sick and welcomes the marginalized to be his closest companions."[10]

God doesn't want a relationship only with the high priests and the religiously "cleaned up." He is also after us ordinary, poor, hungry, lonely, sick, used, and hurting people. God further reveals this in the fact that He announces the birth of His Son to a group of shepherds, the lowliest people in the social/religious caste system. Furthermore, Jesus is born in a stable, wrapped in rags, placed in a feeding trough, and surrounded by cattle. He is present everywhere—even (and maybe especially) in the least desirable of places.

There is no place Jesus refuses to go and there is no life in which Jesus refuses to work. In fact, Jesus often uses the weak and foolish things of the world to shame the strong and wise. There are people the world may label "the least of these" or "Nazarenes." Jesus has a special place among these people: He became one of them. If you want to experience Him today, look for Him there.

---

[10] Steve Chalke, *The Lost Message of Jesus* (Grand Rapids, MI: Zondervan, 2003); 45.

FELLOWSHIP

▼

1 John 1:3 - "We proclaim to you what we have seen and heard, so that you also may have fellowship with us. And our fellowship is with the Father and with his Son, Jesus Christ."

God exists in an eternal relationship: Father, Son, and Holy Spirit. When Christians come together and testify to their life with Jesus, they are joining this fellowship.

Have lunch or coffee with someone today and listen to their story. Ask how you can pray for them and then pray for each other.

▼

1. Why would God send His Son to a peasant family from an unimportant town?
2. What does it feel like to be considered "least" or "nobody"?
3. What did Mary do to warrant the coming of Jesus into her life? What do we do to warrant the coming of Jesus into our lives?
4. Who are the "least of these" in your life? How do you see Jesus in them?
5. What is one tangible way you can serve the least of these this week?

Read Luke 1:26-38, Matthew 25:31-40, and reflect on the week.
What has the Holy Spirit revealed to you this week?

▼

SATURDAY | REST

"The Lord will fight for you, you need only to be still."
- Exodus 14:14

DECEMBER - WEEK FOUR

JESUS AS KING

MONDAY - READ MATTHEW 2:1-13 AND PSALM 45

One of the more entertaining things in my Little League career was watching the base-coaches give signals. They would try to communicate things like "steal a base" or "bunt the ball" with a hand to their belt or a touch to the brim of their hat. Sending these signals to kids in Little League meant they were often misunderstood. I certainly missed my share of signals because I was busy filling my mouth with Big League Chew! I think we can sometimes approach the continuous ways God breaks into our lives the same way we look at baseball team signals. They are hidden or secret, and they are only meant for the insiders—people like clergy, wise men, or those with lots of time on their hands to become "prayer-warriors." And they can be easily missed by those of us distracted by real life or chewing gum.

But what if God's plan for us is simple and transparent? What if He's not hiding, secretive, or speaking in code? What if He's present, constantly communicating, and constantly inviting? I'm afraid we often ignore the obvious will of God because we are convinced we have to seek out some deeper, hidden meaning for our lives. The Christmas story lays it out very clearly: Jesus wants to be king of our hearts. It's as simple as that! The wise men come to worship a king. The magi come in search of a king. Herod plots to kill every boy under two because he is afraid of the birth of a rival king. This language is all over the Christmas story.

To highlight the Kingship of Jesus in the Christmas story, C.S. Lewis looks at the story through the lens of Psalm 45.[11] The writer of this psalm is speaking of the coronation of a righteous king who will restore justice and fight for God. The psalmist anticipates a day when all the nations of earth will come under the reign of this king. It is not much of a jump to see Jesus as this King who ushers in the reign of God.

There is another character in this psalm: the bride, who is called to leave her native country and give herself to the King. This is the Christmas invitation to the Church, the bride of Christ. We are called to leave our patterns and habits and to come under the reign of Christ! Two thousand years ago, a king was born in a manger. Will He be born in you this year?

---

[1] *C.S. Lewis, Reflection on the Psalms. (New York, NY: HarperCollins. 1986); 197-198.*

FELLOWSHIP

▼

1 John 1:3 - "We proclaim to you what we have seen and heard, so that you also may have fellowship with us. And our fellowship is with the Father and with his Son, Jesus Christ."

God exists in an eternal relationship: Father, Son, and Holy Spirit. When Christians come together and testify to their life with Jesus, they are joining this fellowship.

Have lunch or coffee with someone today and listen to their story. Ask how you can pray for them and then pray for each other.

▼

1. Are you more like Herod, who is threatened by Jesus as King, or the wise men who are seeking the King? What makes you say that?
2. What does it mean for Jesus to be the king of your heart?
3. What does repentance mean? How does this relate to making Jesus your king?
4. What is the benefit of making Jesus your king?

Read Matthew 2:1-13, Psalm 45, and reflect on the week.
What has the Holy Spirit revealed to you this week?

SATURDAY | REST

"In peace I will lie down and sleep, for you alone, Lord, make me dwell in safety." Psalm 4:8

EXTRA
5 SUNDAY MONTHS

WATERS THAT DROWN

JESUS AS NEW CREATION

READ GENESIS 1:2-3A, GENESIS 6:17, AND MATTHEW 3:13-17

The baptism of Jesus is a scene that should remind us of Genesis 1. In both stories, there is water, the Spirit of God hovering over the water, and the voice of God speaking into the water. Let's explore Jesus's baptism as a moment of new creation.

"Now, the earth was formless and empty, darkness was over the surface of the deep, and the Spirit of God was hovering over the waters" (Genesis 1:2). "Tohu va Bohu" is the Hebrew phrase usually translated as "formless and empty." This phrase does mean empty, but its primary meaning is something like "difficult to seize."[12] You might think, "Sure, emptiness is difficult to seize because it's empty!" But there's a bit more going on here.

This is the same phrase Isaiah used to describe a city that had been destroyed: "The ruined city lies desolate." [13] It is also the phrase Jeremiah uses when he is announcing judgment from God upon a people who have turned their backs on Him: "I looked at the earth, and it was formless and empty..." [14] In Isaiah's and Jeremiah's passages, there is also a sense of destruction, confusion, and chaos in this phrase. [15] In fact, this emptiness could be described as darkness, and that is exactly how the writer of Genesis describes it: "...darkness was over the surface of the deep."[16]

Genesis isn't the only place we see waters of destruction before we see new creation. Our story has another beginning, one that emerges out of destruction. It starts again with Noah as the water covers the face of the earth. Chaos and destruction have their way in the world, and when the water recedes, God calls Noah forward into a new, purified creation.

With the creation and Noah stories as backdrops, we are poised to notice all kinds of symbolism and nuance to the baptism of Jesus! As the water comes over His face, we are reminded of Noah and how the waters came over the face of the earth to purify and bring about a new creation. This water puts to death all the impurities and clears a path for new creation. As Jesus comes up out of the water, the Spirit of God is hovering over the water and speaking. Jesus is the new Adam, the new creation, the purified human coming up out of the waters of chaos.

---

[12] Francis Brown, Samuel Rolles Driver, and Charles Augustus Briggs, Enhanced Brown-Driver-Briggs Hebrew and English Lexicon (Oxford: Clarendon Press, 1977), 1062. | [13] Isaiah 24:10 NIV | [14] Jeremiah 4:23a | [15] Robert L. Thomas, New American Standard Hebrew-Aramaic and Greek Dictionaries : Updated Edition (Anaheim: Foundation Publications, Inc., 1998). | [16] Genesis 1:2 NIV

MEMORIZE

▼

This week, memorize the following scripture:
"The thief comes only to steal and kill and destroy; I have come that they may have life, and have it to the full."
John 10:10

1. Tell your baptism story. Have you been baptized? Why/Why not? What do you think about baptism?

2. Do you think it's true that some things have to die in order for other things to come to life in you? Why/Why not?

3. What does it mean for something in your life to die? What is an example of something that should "die" in a person's life?

4. What is one thing in your life that you think needs to "die" in order to make room for new life to happen? How can you ensure that thing dies?

5. Have you ever connected baptism with entering Noah's ark? How is Jesus like the ark? How is baptism like "entering" Jesus?

Read Genesis 1:2-3a, Genesis 6:17, Matthew 3:13-17, and reflect on the week.
What has the Holy Spirit revealed to you this week?

SATURDAY | REST

"Be still and know that I am God." Psalm 46:10

WATERS THAT PART

JESUS AND TRUSTING GOD

ONDAY - READ MATTHEW 3:13-17, EXODUS 14:21-22, AND JOSHUA 3:14-17

Imagine the parting of the water as John the Baptist lifts Jesus's head up out of the Jordan River. The water swells, rises to a breaking point, and then falls around the face of Jesus with His eyes closed and His hair soaked. Water gives way to the will of God. This isn't the first time we have seen waters part to allow the future of God to come bursting into the present.

Think back to the story of the Israelites. They have been held as slaves in Egypt, forced to make bricks, and valued for what they could produce for their slave-masters. Moses enters the scene and calls the people out of captivity into the future God has for them. But confusingly, they are led to a giant body of water—impassable, looming between them and their promised future.

Then God parts the water, and a people are born. They walk on dry ground into the future God has prepared for them—to become the people of God on a mission to restore the broken world.

The very next generation faces another body of water between them and God's promises. They find themselves at the bank of the Jordan River at flood stage. On the other side of the river lies the Promised Land. The priests step forward, carrying the Ark, and when they walk into the river, it is held back until the whole nation walks through the parted waters into God's future.

With every story, the people of God have to learn how to trust this God of promise. Imagine walking through a sea trusting that you won't drown. Would God come through for them? Does God really love them and is God really interested in their well-being? With these stories, the Israelites would learn to answer "yes" to those questions!

It wasn't until the water was parted that Jesus heard, "This is my son in whom I am well pleased." Are you willing to put a foot into your fear and learn how to trust God? It may be through taking a risk with the Lord that you will hear "I love you" and "I'm pleased with you." We must pass through the fear of losing our life in order to find it. Jesus invites us to trust God with our whole life as we walk into the mission and future He has for us.

MEMORIZE

▼

This week, memorize the following scripture:
"Come to me, all you who are weary and burdened,
and I will give you rest. Take my yoke upon you and
learn from me, for I am gentle and humble in heart,
and you will find rest for your souls. For my yoke is
easy and my burden is light."
Matthew 11:28-30

▼

1. Do you have any people in your life whom you trust completely? Who?
2. What does a person have to do in order to earn your trust? What does a person have to do in order to break your trust?
3. What does it mean to trust God? Is this difficult for you?
4. Do you believe God has your best interest in mind? Why/Why not?
5. Can you name something in your life (a sin, habit, idea concerning God, etc.) that just won't "part" and allow you to move forward? How would a greater trust in the character of God help you move forward as a person of God?

Read Matthew 3:13-17, Exodus 14:21-22, Joshua 3:14-17, and reflect on the week.
What has the Holy Spirit revealed to you this week?

SATURDAY | REST

"Take my yoke upon you and learn from me, for I am gentle and humble in heart, and you will find rest for your souls." Matthew 11:29

WATERS THAT NAME

JESUS AS PERSONAL

The Gospels are chock full of personal names. It's not by accident that Luke provides a list of names, a genealogy, after Jesus's baptism. It is a way to mark the ministry of Jesus. It is personal and rooted in the soil of the lives of everyday people. Jesus has a name and a family and a history.

Eugene Peterson says, "At our birth, we are named, not numbered." He goes on to say that, "What we are named is not as significant as that we are named."[17] In Luke list of names, we see that God's mission is personal. It includes real people who have a zip code, a culture, friends, and family. The mission of God is something that impacts actual, ordinary people. Here's the thing: God knows their names.
These people who are used to carry forward the mission and promises of God are known. They are not nameless people on a historical canvas. They are recorded. If God knows their names, He can know your name as well.

When we identify with the life of Christ, we take our place in a long line of believers who are known. We aren't seen for merely our potential or usefulness. We are known and named as beloved children of God. Often, we believe that in order to be known we have to create our identity and introduce ourselves. In the people of God, we come to realize that our identity isn't created but bestowed. Some may believe that identifying with Jesus means you lose your personality and your identity is swallowed up in the "Christian" culture. But that is not how God works. In fact, the only way to really find yourself is to lose yourself in Christ. If God is anything, He is personal. Do you want to be known? Do you want a name? Come and abide in Christ. Take your place in the long line of people who carried forward the purposes of God. Then you'll know what it feels like to be known personally by a personal God.

---

[17] Eugene Peterson, *Run With the Horses* (Downers Grove, IL: Intervarsity Press, 2009), 26.

MEMORIZE

▼

This week, memorize the following scripture:
"Then he called the crowd to him along with his disciples and said: "Whoever wants to be my disciple must deny themselves and take up their cross and follow me. For whoever wants to save their life will lose it, but whoever loses their life for me and for the gospel will save it. What good is it for someone to gain the whole world, yet forfeit their soul? Or what can anyone give in exchange for their soul?
Mark 8:34-37

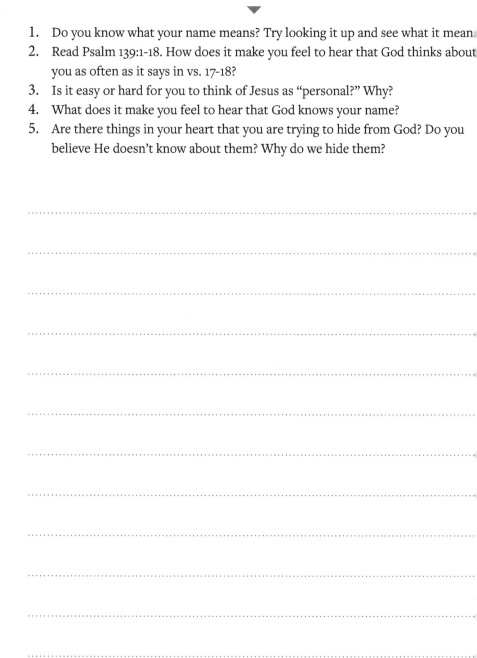

1. Do you know what your name means? Try looking it up and see what it mean.
2. Read Psalm 139:1-18. How does it make you feel to hear that God thinks about you as often as it says in vs. 17-18?
3. Is it easy or hard for you to think of Jesus as "personal?" Why?
4. What does it make you feel to hear that God knows your name?
5. Are there things in your heart that you are trying to hide from God? Do you believe He doesn't know about them? Why do we hide them?

Read Luke 3:23-38, Psalm 139:1-18, Revelation 2:17, and reflect on the week.

What has the Holy Spirit revealed to you this week?

SATURDAY | REST

"Whenever Jesus comes he establishes rest..."
Oswald Chambers

WATER THAT'S GONE

JESUS AS TEMPTED

MONDAY - READ MATTHEW 4:1-2 AND MARK 14:32-51

Right after His baptism, Jesus is led by the Spirit into the desert wilderness. The w ter that was a source of purity, healing, and identity formation during His baptisn gone. Then, to make matters more difficult, Jesus doesn't eat for forty days! Wher the Scripture says that He is hungry, we should read "dying of hunger!" Forty days is thought to be the maximum amount of time a person could go without food. W does Jesus deny Himself a basic human necessity?

While in the desert, Jesus comes face to face with human temptation. That, after all, is why He is led there. Ever since Adam and Eve chose the fruit over obedienc to God, the human body has been mortal. That means that we simply cannot igno the call of our flesh: those temporary things that drag us out of the eternal into th realm of present desires and immediate gratification. It is the power of our flesh that leads us to submit to things like lust, materialism, and indulgence in every wa Our flesh is the source of our temptation.

Therefore, when Jesus denies Himself food, He is practicing the art of denying the flesh. This is the largest benefit to fasting. We develop the habit of turning off the voice of our flesh that leads us to temptation. Fasting, then, is a time of strength-ening the spirit while starving the flesh. We often get a picture of a weak Jesus afte forty days of fasting, but perhaps Jesus was at His strongest!

Fast forward to a garden when He asks His disciples to forego sleep so they could pray with Him. This, by the way, is another form of fasting (denying the "needs" o "desires" of the flesh in order to feed the Spirit). Jesus isn't being cruel here; this not some kind of hazing ritual. In Mark 14:38, we see that Jesus's invitation to stay awake is so His disciples will not fall into temptation. He isn't trying to make then weaker without sleep. He is trying to make them stronger! But the disciples can't stay awake. Their spirit is willing, but their flesh is weak. What happens next is no surprise: They all run away. They aren't quite as practiced as Jesus at denying thei flesh and not strong enough to fight the temptation before them.

MEMORIZE

▼

This week, memorize the following scripture:
*"On hearing this, Jesus said, "It is not the healthy
who need a doctor, but the sick. But go and learn
what this means: 'I desire mercy, not sacrifice.' For I
have not come to call the righteous, but sinners."*
Matthew 9:12-13

1. How would you describe temptation? Have you ever experienced this?
2. What are some common temptations for you—things that seem to keep coming up in your life?
3. How do these temptations hinder you from living the way you want to live?
4. Have you ever practiced fasting? What was your experience?
5. How might fasting help you overcome temptation?

Read Matthew 4:1-2, Mark 14:32-51, and reflect on the week.
What has the Holy Spirit revealed to you this week?

SATURDAY | REST

*"We will never be at rest with less than God's
perfect abundance flowing into us each day."*
Dr. Bud McCord "The Satisfying Life"

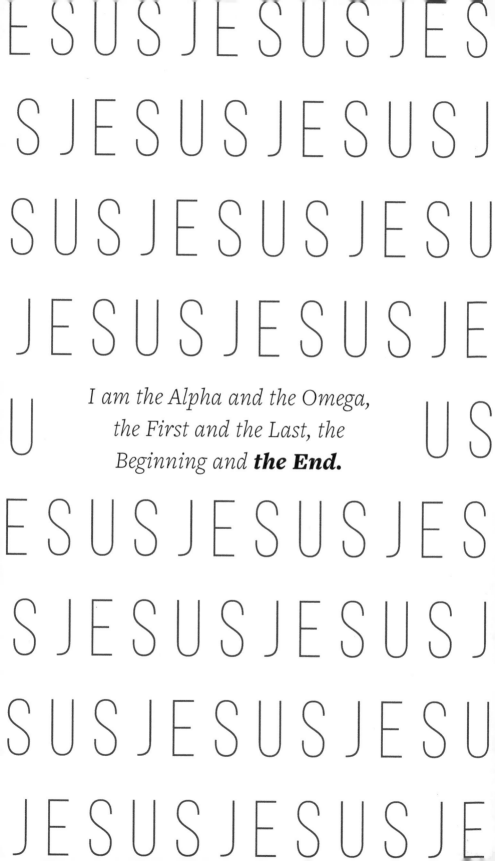

*I am the Alpha and the Omega, the First and the Last, the Beginning and **the End.***

SEE HIM. **LIVE** HIM. **HEAR** HIM. **LOVE** HIM.

Printed in the USA
CPSIA information can be obtained
at www.ICGtesting.com
LVHW071556170424
777699LV00024B/1342